Join Our Family
Social Media Platforms

www.patreon.com/mennetwork1

Subscribe To My YouTube Channel: Male Enlightenment TV

Channel Link:

https://www.youtube.com/channel/UCJ2QanQKgvlCOLuGLb3-b5A?view_as=subscriber

Join Our Facebook Group @ Male Enlightenment Group

https://www.facebook.com/groups/393806287907825/

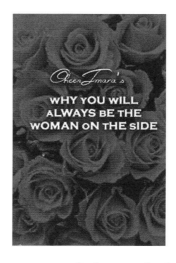

Be Sure To Get Your Copy Of The Book That Started It All

Available On: Amazon.com

Special Thank You To My
Legacy Tier I & Legacy Tier II
PATREON Family

Legacy Tier I

Jham

Lawrence Victor

Legacy Tier II

Jeremiah EL

Phillip Jamison

Special Thanks To My Sponsors:

BlackRam313	Terrence T. Williams
Ill Wills	Goalden Child
Thinking Man's Templar	Kevin Lavere
Muhammed Sokhna	Ambition Matters
Brandon Kwabena	Iso Novoso
Man Friday	Jazz Jackson
Messy Thrills	ThomasTooMuch
Make Africa Great Again (MAGA)	

Young And Successful

The Gentlemen's Book Of Enlightenment (MGTOW/SYSBM Red Pill Guide)

Volume 1
Oheen Imara

Introduction

This book is dedicated to the men of society who have been miseducated and led astray. The men who have been removed from their path and purpose by temptation. The men who were encouraged to ignore their destiny in the pursuit sexual conquest. The men who were indoctrinated into the blue pill mindset to believe their manhood was attached to the number of women they slept with. This is a dedication to all the men who were beat into submission through shaming language and criticism. The men who chased materialism and women only to learn these activities are self-defeating endeavors. The men who fell into depression, drinking, drugs, and harmful activities when they discovered the sobering truth about society. This is for the men who are now trapped on the plantation of alimony and/or child support. The men who feel like their situation is hopeless and believe they are alone. My hope is you gentlemen will see yourself in these writings and use this information to follow your true purpose. That you will understand, her behavior is not caused by or a reflection of you. That you will understand that is her nature and if it were not you it would have been another guy. I want men to understand that once they walk away from the belief that you need to be with a woman to be complete a new world of possibility appears. Once you reject the word "Love" in terms of relationships and accept there is only respect everything changes.

I want men to understand that she does not love you, she loves what you can do for her. She does not see you as a man, she sees you as a utility to be used and discarded when what she believes is a better utility comes along. When you understand these truths, you can walk away from the mental prison that society has created for you. You will be enlightened and focus on your true purpose. When you are enlightened to the truth you will never carry hatred, disdain, or scorn for women you will simply understand them. This knowledge will protect you from the many traps that are placed on your path in your journey to true peace and happiness.

MGTOW & SYSBM
The False Narrative Our Ideology Promotes Hate

As you gentlemen have already gathered our movement is being attacked on all levels. The weapon that is being used to disseminate this false information regarding the male space is Social Media, Television, Film, Music, Corporations, Government, and of course Women. All these entities operate in unison to provide a false representation of our ideology. Billions of dollars and thousands of hours have been invested in misrepresenting our beliefs and true intentions. As you know, the shaving company Gillette which is owned by Procter & Gamble initiated an attack on masculinity with a controversial ad campaign titled "We believe: The Best Men Can Be". The ad depicted men in a very negative light and placed masculinity on trial in the commercial that lasted one minute and fifty seconds. The propaganda hit piece faced a great deal of backlash because it depicted all men as mindless Neanderthals who held no respect for women and behaved like savages. It was a dark depiction of masculinity and made it appear as if being male was a disease.

Men all over the country if not the world were outraged at the implications of this ad campaign and walked away from the Gillette brand. Based on their audacity, insensitivity, and willful ignorance, the company would go on to lose over 8 billion dollars in revenue. The film industry would embark on their own misinformation ad campaign providing the masses with films that depicted men as idiots, losers, weirdos, insecure, weak, and even violent. Hollywood has ramped up its propaganda campaign to make women the stars of films they do not even have interest in. This is evidenced by the box office bombs that have failed in dramatic fashion. In these films, men are the patriarchy, the abusers who only seek to marginalize women. While this message may resonate with a small fraction of the population, many films and television shows have been cancelled or failed to make back its budget.

The media has contributed to the propaganda as well with various articles falsely linking the ideologies of "Men Going Their Own Way" as well as "Save Yourself Black Men" to hatred of women. These articles paint a portrait of men that wish to walk away from the western culture version of courtship, dating, co-habitation, and marriage as losers. We live in our parent's basements, work minimum wage jobs, masturbate to pornography, and lack the ability to attract the opposite sex. They have invested a great deal of resources to ensure that men who walk away from a societal structure that demonizes them and take advantage of their contributions are labeled Incels. If you do not part with your resources by way of child support and alimony, If you do not allow women to move in your home or provide them with tangibles society labels you as a man that hates women. While this is an extreme declaration it is necessary for this society to survive. What we must understand is that this civilization is based on the sacrifice of men. You have been bred to sacrifice your happiness, sanity, and even your life so the rest of society can prosper. That would be perfectly fine if men were shown appreciation for their sacrifices, however this is not the case. Instead of praise they receive ridicule, instead of appreciation they receive condemnation. The society benefits from men living in ignorance and maintaining a perpetual state of obscurity. Keeping men in the dark and preventing them from recognizing their impact is necessary to maintain the function of the status quo. MGTOW and SYSBM is a direct threat to this archaic system because it seeks to liberate the minds of men.

The onslaught of verbal assaults, misinformation, and propaganda are designed to conceal the reality that men are the lifeblood of any society. We can use the example of government or a major corporation. The government and the corporation present a grand picture of themselves with strong logos, advertisement, and slogans. They appear powerful and all knowing, never to be questioned or viewed with doubt. They tell you what you need, what you are entitled to and what you should have and many of us fall for this extravagant illusion. Government Tells you banks need a bailout, or the republic will collapse. Apple says you will never be able to survive without an iPhone or iMac. Amazon and Google tell you that you will never be able to function without Alexa or Google Assistant. They present the situation in this manner because they never want you to understand the truth of the matter. They never want you to discover that you are their means of survival, they depend on you. Their presentation is the reverse to make you believe that you would perish without them, but the reality is they do not survive without you.

If people suddenly rose in one voice and rejected government, refused to pay taxes, refused to participate in elections what could the government do to stop all its citizens. How many could they imprison or kill before they were absolutely toppled? If people stopped buying Apple products and decided they no longer wanted to support the company would it continue to be a trillion-dollar company? What if people no longer wanted those personal assistant items in their home, how would that affect Google and Amazon? If all the things I just mentioned were to happen you would then see the reality that all these entities need you. Most of all they need your ignorance. The government needs you to believe you need them and your taxes go to roads, schools, and services. Apple needs you to believe you need the next iPhone despite the fact it is the same exact phone as the previous year's model with a new number. Google and Amazon need you to believe you would be lost without their personal assistant.

The truth is government would die if they did not steal your money. Apple would fall apart if you never brought another product. Google and Amazon would disappear if you no longer purchased their products. Your money and ignorance keep these businesses going and they work very hard to keep it that way.

The same is true with women. They are selling a product of companionship, dating, relationship, marriage, and children. Just like the corporations they present an image; you will not survive without our products. Like the government and corporations, they seek to present a picture doom and gloom without their product. Like the government and corporations, women depend on your money and your ignorance. Women need you to purchase the products of dating, relationships, marriage, and children to secure and improve their financial standing. This method has allowed them to fool the customer into thinking they are worthless without their products. For generations and even today this has been the method of transferring wealth from a man to his female counterpart.

"Men Going Their Own Way" or "Black Man Save Yourself" are ideologies that are in complete opposition of an institution that has benefitted women for ages. The natural reaction for women is to fight against the changing of this system and their weapon is manipulation and shaming. When a man claims "MGTOW" or "SYSBM" women need you to see three types of men: 1) The Incel 2) The Financially Unattractive 3) Men Who Hate Women.

The Incel

If you have decided to walk away from dating and relationships women want people to view you as an Incel. This term describes a man that is physically unattractive, exhibits weird behaviors, an introvert, awkward, and lacks social skills. He lives alone not because he enjoys the peace and solitude but because he lacks the ability to interact with women. He is seen as creepy or odd and makes women feel uncomfortable. He is either scrawny or obese and most likely a nerd. men who walk away from the dating and relationship scene receive this label because it will immediately explain your withdrawal without raising suspicion or drawing attention to your cause. If you are labeled an Incel, your reasons for leaving dating and relationships are ignored and dismissed. When women and blue pill men classify you as an Incel it sends a message to everyone that you are simply a loser who cannot compete against better more qualified men. If this propaganda is disseminated successfully no one will inquire about a man's withdrawal they will assume he is just unworthy. In more extreme cases it will push that man back into dating and relationships to avoid the stigma placed on him.

The Financially Unattractive

Another label that has been placed on men who has walked away from the traps and pitfalls of dating and relationships is being financially unattractive. This label implies that he has walked away from the dating/relationship scene because he does not possess the financial resources to sustain a relationship. This label gives the perception the man withdrew because he is broke. He is unable to pay for dates or pursue courtship which means that he will be unable to provide for a family, so he is disqualified. This is yet another tactic utilized to explain a man's withdrawal from the current state of dating so men and women that are still participating in this system do not become alarmed. Women hear the term "financially unattractive" and think if he cannot buy a house, a car, pay for dates, pay for clothes, pay for trips, give me money, or access to his accounts he is worthless. They immediately dismiss him as well as his reason for abandoning the dating market. The thought of a man lacking financial resources makes him irrelevant and any issues he may have, becomes mute. This makes him a loser and his reputation is shattered. This tactic is utilized and, in many cases, very effective to diffuse the interest in the ideology of MGTOW or SYSBM.

Men Who Hate Women

Another label men will encounter when they become enlightened and understand the true essence of female nature, is the asinine notion that they hate women. This is yet another tactic employed by women to diffuse any logical arguments or criticism men may have against modern dating and relationships. The goal of this tactic is to label men as misogynist because this will totally invalidate anything you have to say. Once again, just like the two previous groups you lack the ability to attract and, in many cases, satisfy women which is why you hate them. This is an excellent tactic because it completely distracts from the issue at hand and places a label on the individual seeking to express his position. Any issues you have with modern dating is now labeled hate speech and you are suddenly placed in a category with dangerous hate groups and teased for your perceived inadequacies. This is probably the biggest misconceptions about the Male Space also known as Men Going Their Own Way or Save Yourself Black Man is that we have hatred for women.

All three of these labels are created and utilized by women for the purpose to ensure their survival. The goal is manipulation, confusion, and in some cases chaos to ensure that men continue to participate in the losing game of dating, relationships, marriage and co-habitation. A man's inability to see, impaired judgement, and willful ignorance is the necessary recipe to ensure that women are financially secure without the responsibility of providing anything in return. The Fact that men are Going Their Own Way and Saving Themselves is a sign that they are losing control of their stock. Suddenly men have awakened to the realities of what these archaic institutions believe and practice. With this new knowledge, men no longer want to participate. While shaming language and labels are unable to bring men, who are enlightened back to the plantation, the hope is to prevent the current group of slaves from defecting. The goal is to prevent future generations of men from deciding to take the red pill and walk the true path of enlightenment.

This is absolutely a false representation of our ideology and belief system. The enlightened man who has embraced the red pill does not seek to express hatred or disdain for the opposite sex, we simply seek to understand them. As enlightened men of this ideology we remove emotion from the analysis of female nature and behavior because such endeavors are counterproductive and dangerous. Men who react on emotion as opposed to verified insight and information are likely to respond in an illegal, immoral, and unethical manner. The men of this ideology acknowledge it is the male with the "Blue Pill" mindset that will indulge in the ignorance of emotions. The "Blue Pill" man, the man who refuses to embrace the reality of a red pill society is the one who is jealous and insecure. Blue-pilled men want to know where she is and what she is doing. The blue-pilled man leaves one-hundred messages on her phone and many more text. The "Blue-pilled" man is the man that becomes violent and will physically assault or harm women. The Blue-pilled man will become emotional and feel no other recourse but to attack a woman out of anger and rage. Blue-pilled men are also the men who will take a woman's life and cowardly take their own in the process. The need to immediately react and become emotional is not a red pill characteristic. It is directly in line with the behaviors you would expect from women.

To label this male space anything other than a philosophical ideology, a belief system, or a sense of enlightenment is willful ignorance. It is a diversionary tactic done purposely to remove any legitimacy our ideology has acquired. Our perception of societal norms has, by default made us a subculture because we reject the progressive or liberal mindset. This is of course dangerous to a system that is completely dependent of the ignorance and servitude of men, so they label those who walk outside of the agenda societal outlaws. The man that refuses to bow to the gynocracy and worship the feminine structure is rejecting the archaic system of mental slavery which also confirms that government can no longer use him. The enlightened man that walks away from the traps of dating, relationships, co-habitation, and marriage cannot be held as debt slave. The enlightened man will not be trapped by the prisons of Alimony, Child Support, Anniversaries, Holidays, Date Nights, Vacations, Birthday's, Mortgages, Car Notes, Credit Cards and other traps that Women and Government have placed in your path. Men Going Their Own Way and Save Yourself Black Men are labeled as hate groups because they are a danger to the system set in place to ensure your slavery and this should enhance your dedication to following these ideologies.

What Does She Have To Offer You?

(What Does She Bring To The Table?)

She sat across the table from me trying to think of what she could possibly say to persuade me to resume a relationship with her. We were together for five years and it suddenly ended when she decided to be unfaithful with a man she had met at her job. Not only did she decide to sleep with another man, but she wanted me to know of her misdeeds. She would leave the house on that that day at 12pm and would not return until the next day at 2:40am. Anyone in a relationship understands that behavior like this is a declaration of war and should be treated as such. I'm sure she wanted a reaction, but the reality is I fell out of infatuation with her a year before the infidelity. When I met her, I was a bachelor with a two-bedroom apartment in very nice part of the North Bronx in New York City. I was dating and enjoying being single, but it was something about her that made me give up my freedom. I am ashamed to say I allowed the blue-pilled beta and arrogance in me to take control and proceeded to fall under her spell.

The reality is that she was a bum. She had absolutely nothing and she was nothing to look at to add. She had a tacky short haircut with worn out clothing and shoes with no laces. She was a little overweight and her teeth were discolored. No one paid her any attention she was invisible where we worked. To add to this, she lived with her grandmother on the south side of the Bronx which is the definition of poverty. Of course, all these things are warning signs, but my arrogance would blind me to what was directly in front of me. Now the question many of you may ask is why did I select her? As I said I was successful and had a steady rotation of women at my disposal. I did not need this woman in my life, and I could have simply made her another chick in the rotation. The reason I selected this woman was because she was very young and appeared to be a blank canvas. While I held no illusions of virginity or chastity, I felt that her experiences were limited. She was a freshman to life and relationships and I arrogantly decided that I would play the role of God to this peasant woman.

With that conceited mindset, I proceeded to change her life. I was successful and she would benefit in every way. I helped her lose weight, purchased her a new wardrobe, and even helped grow her hair far below her shoulders. I even helped her with the teeth whitening process. I took this nobody and made her important. She was invisible during her tenure where we were employed and suddenly, she became the most important person in the building. Men that ignored her wanted to be with her and women wanted to be her. I made this woman what I wanted her to be and proceeded to enjoy the fruits of my labor. Unfortunately, I lost myself in the process. I had fell in love with my creation and lost control of the situation.

I now had this young beautiful lady and she hypnotized me. She knew that I was under her spell and she proceeded to take advantage.

Anything she wanted was made available to her and her taste had begun to grow. She graduated from shoes, clothes, sporting events and Broadway shows to wanting to move out of the state and purchasing a home. I was under her spell and I made this happen. I brought her a beautiful home in North Carolina and shortly after we moved, we learned the hard way that she needed a vehicle. I taught her how-to drive-in New York and helped her get a license so we went to a dealership and I placed a sizable down payment on a brand-new vehicle for her and placed her under my car insurance. Just like that, this bum who slept on her grandmother's couch on the poor side of town became a very attractive, homeowner, and new driver in a completely different state. I had visions of making a family with this woman and building a life. Based on this mindset I completely missed that I had either created or fed a narcissistic, manipulative, and selfish monster. I was willing to give her a home, a car, access to my credit cards, a joint bank account, clothing, shoes, and gifts. All I wanted in return... was for her to keep the home I purchased for her clean. Despite all the things she was given she could never do that for me.

We had many conversations on this topic but no matter how many times we discussed it she could never complete this task. I remember a time when I stayed home from work because we had a pile of dishes in the kitchen. She would refuse to clean these dishes despite the fact we had a dishwashing machine. I remember placing the dishes in the machine and cleaning the rest of the house while the machine did all the work. I thought to myself "She couldn't even place the dishes in the machine and press the start button?". As time went on and we continued to have these disagreements, it became clear that this woman did not love me. I had to accept the reality she was not in love with me, she loved the things I did for her. This was merely a theory when I initially had the thought however, it would be proven during one of our disagreements where she stated in no uncertain terms "I will either cook or clean but I'm not doing both". This was when I knew my Frankenstein monster had turned against me. This bum from the Bronx who was homeless and slept on her grandmother's couch was giving me ultimatums. Her spell had begun to break but it completely shattered when she failed to honor her own agreement and made a statement like "Well I think we have a difference of opinion". Just like that, the love goggles fell off and I was now able to see her for who she was. From that moment on I did not love her I just tolerated her. I can honestly say I stayed because I did not have the guts to just end the relationship.

We moved back to New York City, but I kept the house in North Carolina and rented it out. I returned to NYC because we did not fully consider that the economy in North Carolina was terrible. I was offered a six-figure salary to return and I could not pass on the opportunity. However, our return to the city was when things really began to unravel. Suddenly she was on social media, then she had male friends, and finally she wanted to have girl's night out. These were all things we initially agreed were a violation of our relationship but now here she was breaking all the rules. Which leads us to the day she left at 12:30pm and returned the next day at 2:40am. To be honest I didn't even care that she cheated I was more upset that she used a cellphone that I brought her and a phone plan that I paid for to call and text him. I was more upset that she used a car that I helped her pay for and my car insurance to drive around with him. I was more upset that she used clothes and shoes that I paid for. I didn't even care about where she was or what she did. I did not even have the urge to call her that evening and I was unaware of the time she came in the house. She had to tell me the time she arrived, and I didn't even ask. The way I learned of her infidelity was through one of her so-called friends. Her story was that they went out for drinks and hung out for 15 hours and 40 minutes and she was positive that her friend would confirm the events she described.

She was so confident that her friend would corroborate her story she places me and the female on the phone. To her surprise the friend told me the truth that she was in fact with another man. Our relationship ended right there. She used the break-up to reacquaint herself with bad habits. She began drinking and smoking marijuana as well as sleeping with different men. I stayed focused. I went to the gym and began eating properly as well as saving money. One day she invites me out to eat so we can talk which led us to this moment where we are sitting at this table and she is trying to figure out what to say. "So, what can I do to make this right?" she asked. Even in her defeat she could not be graceful, she didn't even want to make me feel important. She did not want to acknowledge that she destroyed something great, she just wanted it back with minimal effort. To her I am the beta so she believes that she can say "My Fault" and everything can go back to normal. Unfortunately for her she is missing some critical points. As I sit across from her looking at her stupid face, she does not understand I do not love her and have not for at least a year and a half. I'm am not sitting here because I am nostalgic, I am here because I am entertained, and it is a free meal.

"What?" I asked her confused.

"What do I have to do to fix our situation?" She responded.

It had suddenly become clear. In her haste to abandon this relationship she completely ignored that she was in the best position possible. She was a homeowner, built a portfolio, had access to funds and credit, and the had someone to take care of her bills. She became bored with comfort and safety and threw it all away for a life of drugs, drinking, and promiscuity. The problem of course being is after you are used up and passed around, after everyone has had their turn, after new becomes old you are left with nothing but a used up, beat up vagina. You're not the new girl anymore and the calls stop. So here she is trying to get in my good graces and doing a terrible job at that. She wanted me to forget that several dudes had most likely got blowjobs and placed their member in several holes. She wanted me to forget that she cheated and lied. She wanted me to forget that she was extremely disrespectful and take her back now that all those guys had their fun with her for free. Now that they were done, she wanted me to pay for what she had given away. I asked her a question that revolutionized my thought process and forever changed the way I think about women. It made me look at the world in a totally different light.

I said the following "If I take you back, you get access to a home, You get access to my six figure salary, my credit cards, my bank accounts, you get your bills paid. You get the comfort and protection of a relationship, and financial security. You get the ability to travel and experience new things. You get gifts on holidays, birthdays, and anniversaries. You get new clothes, new shoes, and jewelry. You get your hair and nails done... Tell me... What do I get in return for providing this?"

It was at that moment I believe her entire world came crashing down. I believe this was the moment she realized that her mental manipulation, her ability to control the narrative had died. She was no longer looking at someone who had loved her and cared deeply for her. She was facing a man with the alpha mindset. The man she was looking for had been buried the night I learned she cheated and there was no possibility of resurrection. She is looking at a completely different individual who has no investment in a future with her. She is on the other side of the table trying to think of something to say but she can muster any words. Finally, she can utter three words "I love you" to which I smiled and respond, "I thought we agreed we were not going to lie to one another?". This was the moment I realized the truth and that truth is... **She Has Nothing To Offer You**. For our entire lives we live in a fog completely oblivious to the reality that she has absolutely nothing to offer us. Men have worked their fingers to the bone, suffered and even died to provide women with comfort, safety, and financial stability only to be blinded to the reality that she offers nothing in return. Men are told by the society that they must provide a foundation of stability, financial support, protection, and resources. They are told that they must work and toil to generate income and establish value. A man is required to provide and to constantly re-establish himself in order to remain relevant. However, we have never thought to ask, what do women have to offer? What does she provide? How does she contribute to a relationship or marriage? We have been distracted from asking that question because the answer is scary and shocking. To ponder this question is to learn the reality that she has nothing to offer you.

Women despise the question "What Do You Bring To The Table?" because it diminishes their control and power over the direction of a relationship. Asking that question is a clear indicator that you will not be manipulated or controlled which destroys the purpose of a relationship for the modern woman. Asking a woman what she brings to the table disarms her ability to control you and reveals that she is nothing more than a parasite leaching off the accomplishments and the success of the male host. She digs her tentacles into the body of her male host mentally controlling him. She burrows deep into his brain disarming his ability to fight or use rational thought to make informed decisions. She wants money, she wants to go shopping, she wants jewelry, she wants to travel, she wants to go to the beauty salon. But what do you get in return for financing her life? Nothing, financing her lifestyle does not even buy her loyalty or respect. To her your servitude is merely an entitlement that is owed to her. The fact that men are now accepting our ideology and are asking this question has created a disturbance in the gynocracy.

The question itself reveals the truth that you are aware, alert, and understand that she has absolutely nothing to offer. The source of her power is your ignorance to this fact. She expects you to provide tangible items while she provides abstract attributes. As a man you are expected to provide a home, transportation, protection, financial incentives, leisure and entertainment, food, travel expenses, a portion of your income, as well your time to maintain a relationship. She wants you to provide concrete benefits for you to enter and remain in a relationship. To add to this, you are required to constantly re-establish your position on a regular basis as a condition for the relationship to continue.

However, her response for you providing concrete tangibles is to offer you abstract benefits. If you ask a woman what she brings to the table, she will answer you with things you are unable to quantify. She will say something like she can provide you with "Companionship", "Emotional Support", or "Love". None of these things have any tangible or quantifiable value and are not based in guarantees. Whenever she feels like it, she has the right to withdraw her emotional support, companionship, and love at any time. When she decides to vacate the relationship her abstract contributions to the relationship go with her. However, when men provide tangible concrete benefits, he is unable to withdraw his contributions to the relationship. It is not as easy for a man to withdraw a home, vehicle, or financial support when he leaves the relationship. For generations men have been bamboozled into helping women improve their financial and social standing with no guarantees for the men who have made this possible. Men have lifted women out of poverty and have given them the ability to participate in activities they would have never been able access while receiving nothing in return. She has nothing to offer you, but she demands everything you have to give. She will try to justify her existence by saying she gives you children or sex, but the enlightened man understands how critical his participation is in the above-mentioned activities. Your semen is needed just as much as her egg is needed to create that child. Your erection is needed just as much as her feminine moisture is needed to prevent friction. Your sexual gyration is required just as much as hers which means we are back to the original statement, what does she have to offer?

Men have been led astray by the propaganda machine of government, film, and media to believe they are obligated to provide a woman with monetary and materialistic rewards simply for being a woman and having a vagina. On the other hand, we have been conditioned to expect nothing in return. Society has done everything in its power to make sure that we never ask the questions "What Does She Bring To The Table?" or "What Does She Have To Offer?" because it is that moment when the con is exposed. If you think about this as it relates to your life the concept becomes simple. Think about any of your previous relationships. When that relationship ended what did you lose? You paid for the dates, you paid the rent/mortgage, you paid the bills, you paid for her clothing and shoes, you paid to get her hair and nails done. You probably paid for her car note and car insurance not to mention her phone bill. So, what have you really lost when she has decided to leave? What did she provide you with that you are unable to acquire for yourself? What task did she complete that you would be lost without? When you think about this, you are unable to answer these questions because the reality is that she provided nothing in the relationship while you provided everything. The red pill mindset has exposed this truth and has disrupted the system of servitude. As I previously stated, when men recognize their value and walk away from the old system that orchestrated the rules for dating and marriage women begin to lose their power. The question "What do you have to offer?" is a clear indication of this fact. The question forces her to investigate the mirror and realize she is nothing but a leech living off the success of others. Even the so-called independent woman is nothing more than a parasite. She is college educated, has a career, and is supposed to be economically stable and even with all of this she still looks at a man to pay for the date. This is because being a parasite is her default setting. She is always looking to extract resources from men while offering nothing in return.

This is a very important fact that you must consider before you enter a relationship. If you decide to date, cohabitate, or even marry you must understand that the modern woman serves no purpose. She is a trophy or a pretty paper weight with no real contributions to a relationship. Like an expensive vehicle she will catch the eye of many people but the maintenance and upkeep will be very expensive and at some point you will be forced to acknowledge that it is not a benefit it is a liability. She is not interested in building something with you she is more concerned with what she can get from you and in return you will receive nothing. If you want to save yourself a lifetime of pain and heartache, the next woman that wants you to make a commitment to her ask her this simple question "What do you have to offer?". Watch her disappear from your life. Once you ask the question, she will understand that you have taken the red pill and you are awake which means she is unable to control you. Once she learns this reality, she will have no use for you because she has nothing to offer you.

You Will Never Make Her Happy

One of the most important things the male population has failed to recognize in modern society is the reality YOU WILL NEVER MAKE HER HAPPY. Many men have found themselves incarcerated, homeless, and have even committed suicide in the futile attempt to do so. We have been mis-educated by a society who only see men as disposable utilities. We spend our entire lives in service to the government and women in the hopes that we will someday crack the code. However, it takes a lifetime to discover you will never find success pursuing this path. You have spent years placing yourself in a position to become a good provider. You went to college or vocational school because you were taught your chances of meeting a quality woman greatly improved with your success. You thought if you owned a beautiful home and drove a luxury vehicle, she would marvel at your ability to provide and be yours forever. She would bare your children and ensure that your home was clean, and a nutritious meal was prepared when you arrived from a tough day at work. You thought she would appreciate the fact that you were doing all of this for her.

Instead of chasing your true dreams you chained yourself to a desk for forty hours a week and committed to this for thirty to forty years. You did this to provide her with a lifestyle she had grown accustomed to and to keep her happy. However, you quickly learn that everything you have sacrificed is for nothing when she serves you divorce papers, or you find that she is sleeping around. You of course are always the last to know making statements like "I Thought We Were Happy?". This is because men have been conditioned by television, film, family, and government to place the needs of women above our own. Men have been conditioned to believe in self-sacrifice. For example, if the plane is going down or the boat is sinking, you are conditioned to give your parachute or safety vest to your wife or the nearest female. You are taught that women are made of sugar and spice and everything nice while you are made from the worst ingredients. Your entire life has been designed to perform a task that you will never be successful at and when it fails you are taught it is your fault. You thought that being able to provide material items would keep her satisfied, you thought being able to take her on trips to different parts of the world would keep her faithful and by your side. Unfortunately, if you are a part of the male population you have learned many times that there is nothing you can do to make her happy. The biggest mistake a man can make whenever a woman say's "She is not happy" is believe that this statement has something to do with him. As men, we are quick to blame ourselves because she suddenly does not want to "play-house" anymore. We start to look for imperfections in ourselves to justify why she suddenly wants to abandon us. We say stupid things like "Maybe if I was taller, If I made more money, If I drove a better car, she would be happy".   Of course, this is not the case and our lack of understanding as men keeps us from truly comprehending the nature of women.

You are not the issue, and nothing is wrong with you gentlemen. You are the same man you were when you met her. Women will have you doubting yourself and paying pick-up- artist and looking at "how to videos" on YouTube in the hopes of reinventing yourself when the reality of your situation is staring you right in your face.   You Will Never Make Her Happy and if you do not believe that then look at the celebrities and athletes that continue to face divorce and break-ups.   I could go on for the entirety of this book, but I wish to make the point clear. The celebrities are most times considered attractive, wealthy, successful and many of the other attribute's women claim make them happy and yet they continue to face divorce.   As men you must understand, it does not matter how much money you make, how tall you are, how big your penis is, or how strong you are. Eventually you will learn that none of this makes them happy. We have failed to recognize this one vital component and have sacrificed our happiness and mental stability in the process. However, the "Alpha" "Bad Boy" or "Thug" has been successful when dealing with the opposite sex. This is because these types of men have rejected the programming and pursue their own happiness. We can attach negative attributes to these types of men, but they seem to attract women because they understand You Will Never Make Her Happy, so they do not even attempt to or care to do so. These men understand that the female emotions are fleeting so they get what they can out of them and when they no longer have anything to offer, they leave.

As children we were taught to despise the concept of the "PIMP". We were taught that these types of men were the lowest of the low and we should not aspire to be like them. We were taught that these types of men took advantage of these poor unsuspecting women. For a very long time I believed this and failed to understand the true science of pimpology. Pimps and Alphas understand that a key aspect of women is the fact that they thrive in chaos, confusion, uncertainty, and danger.

An article titled, Eight Reasons Women Stay in Abusive relationships by Jason Whiting for the Institute for Family Studies best describes this behavior. According to Mr. Whiting's article women remain in abusive relationships for the following reasons:

1) Distorted Thoughts

2) Damaged Self-Worth

3) Fear

4) Wanting to Be A Savior

5) Children

6) Family Expectations and Experiences

7) Financial Constraints

8) Isolation

While all of these are valid, I believe social scientist must look deeper and recognize that all eight of these reasons provide the excitement that women seek. These reasons acknowledge that women are more likely to stay in abusive relationships. Rational people are inclined to ask why would a woman remain in an abusive relationship when there are so many options available for her to leave? It is because the chaos, uncertainty, and danger are exciting. Never knowing what will happen next is a turn-on for most women. Dr. Vinita Mehta speaks on this matter in her article "Why Do Women Fall for Bad Boys" for Psychology Today. The Article begins with the author asking: Are women predisposed to find men with dark personalities attractive? She continues to answer the question by stating: Indeed, research has established that Dark Triad men demonstrate more sexual success by comparison to their peers. These articles understand that men who have mastered the truth and understanding that they will never make a woman happy are far more successful.

Prostitution just like infidelity and abusive men are areas that are filled with all the above-mentioned characteristics. A pimp provides women with excitement and danger which is why despite the abuse and the mistreatment a woman will stay. The same is true with infidelity. The idea of being caught cheating and the trouble that will most likely follow because of it provides that danger and uncertainty which is why many women are starting to participate in the act. The opposite is true when discussing the gentlemen. The gentlemen provide safety, comfort, stability and women find these things boring. Women view knowing that a man is faithful and will consistently provide as a negative as opposed to a positive.

The truth is all around us, but we choose not to see it because we were raised to be servants and slaves. Just like the young woman who I literally plucked out of poverty. She had lived in a room and ended up sleeping on her grandmother's couch. I was living the bachelor's lifestyle and really had no business being involved with a woman like that. However, I foolishly believed if I became a Captain Save Em All Day and provided her with the lifestyle she was not accustomed to she would appreciate this and reciprocate by making me happy. I took her to Broadway

Shows, Professional Sporting Events, paid for shoes and clothing. I moved her from her grandmother's couch to my two-bedroom apartment in the North Bronx. She would later express interest in owning a home and I would oblige her. She needed a car and I purchased that as well. This was what I believed to be an investment in her happiness and the key to building a foundation for family and marriage. I wanted her to know that I could provide for her and our children in the future.

My belief was showing this woman who came from nothing, who brought nothing to the table, that I could provide, and she would in return appreciate me. I provided her with all these gifts and worked hard to provide her with anything she wanted and in return I only wanted her to keep the house I brought her clean. I quickly learned while she was happy in the moment eventually all these things would lose their appeal and suddenly... she was not happy. While I am not wealthy by any means I knew she was being provided with more than she would ever be able to experience. She fed me sob stories about how past boyfriends treated her like garbage and never got her anything. I wanted to be different, however with all the things I provided she was not happy. My mistake was giving her anything. I should have forced her through some grueling test to see if she was worthy. Of course, the way I was conditioned by society kicked in and I found myself caring about what she needed first and that is the biggest mistake any man could make. I believe my relationship with this woman failed because I attempted to make her happy and this is the recipe for failure. Look at all the men who have adopted the MGTOW lifestyle listen to their stories. It will always begin with these men placing a woman's happiness before their own. Lavishing the woman with attention, time, money, and gifts they do not deserve. You will hear them discuss how they have sacrificed, worked multiple jobs, went into debt, lost relationships all to make some woman happy. Once a man has completed everything, she has requested you will find that she wishes to leave because she is not happy.

What we are attempting to do here is fight against our programming of being "Simps" "Beta-Males" and "Cuckolds" We have to understand when Hollywood produces a romantic comedy or a love story they are attempting to invoke the programming embedded in your brain. They want you to watch films like "The Notebook" or "Valentine's Day" because these films call to your subconscious and tell you that you must jump through hoops and do whatever she request. Music like "When I Get Home" by Babyface or "Baby Come Back" by player send the male brain messages that he should conform to female expectations and live to serve her. The evidence of course is the fact you celebrate holidays and anniversaries. She wants to go places you do not care for but all that matters is what she wants.

You wear clothes you do not even like because she wants to dress you. We do all these things in the hopes that she will appreciate the gestures and recognize what we are willing to do but we learn the hard way You Will Never Make Her Happy. As I previously stated the concept of attempting to make women happy is equivalent to banging your head against a wall and the consequences can potentially lead to your death. A man who is unable to fully comprehend or process this information may resort to actions that are not healthy. They will blindly believe that they are somehow responsible for her behavior instead of understanding that is just who she is and ultimately harm themselves.

I am reminded of a former co-worker who was married to an older woman. Over the years I worked with him, I noticed that his behavior had begun to change drastically. He went from a lively, energetic, social individual to a very introverted type person. I would later leave that job and pursue another career, but I would occasionally receive updates about this co-worker. He spent his last days burying himself into his work until one day he was found in the Hudson river with his seat belt still buckled. It turned out that his wife was not happy, and she showed him by kicking him out of his home and bringing another man into the house around his daughter. In his attempt to make her happy he blamed himself for her evil vindictive ways and in a state of loneliness he decided to end it all. He did not understand that her misery had nothing to do with him and because he was such a happy and positive individual, she sought to destroy his optimism. He failed to recognize that his attempts to make her happy would never yield any success. He did what many men had done and blamed himself for her behavior and allowed these feelings to consume him. I was deeply saddened by the news and it also made me think about the mental anguish he must have experienced now he decided to take his own life.

This man was in so much pain at the thought of his wife being unhappy. She kicked him out of his home to bring another man into the residence. He must have thought all of this was his fault and she would have never resorted to this if he were a better person. This is the subliminal messaging that is triggered at these moments. Those sad love songs where you beg the woman to come back and you will do anything to make things right. I think about the fact that this man was led to believe he was a failure. As the water rushed over his face, he fought the natural instincts of his body to stay alive and allowed himself to drown. All of this happened because he failed to understand You Will Never Make Her Happy.

WHAT SHOULD YOU DO?

We must understand that the belief of making a woman happy is foolish. You will ultimately find that they are irrational and their wants and wishes can suddenly change based on how they feel. Knowing this, it's important to focus on you. Do not allow yourself to be concerned with what she wants because it will cause you to lose focus of what really matters... you. You will find that if you do not heed this advice you will be miserable, unfulfilled and in debt. The foundation of their happiness is built on quicksand and is always sinking. Women seek to deter you from this practice and attempt to use shaming language and refer to you as selfish. They want you to believe that they can be satisfied you are just not trying hard enough and lure you into spending a lifetime jumping through hoops in the hopes of completing an impossible task. You can be the tallest man, make the most money, have the biggest house, Be the most handsome with the longest penis, be the most romantic, and the most loving and she will still find a reason to leave you because, YOU WILL NEVER MAKE HER HAPPY

Single Mothers Are For Desperate Men Only

In the wild, when a male lion conquers the previous regime and inherits the territory as well as the pride. The first thing, he does is kill the cubs of the previous leader. This may appear barbaric and many people may describe it as savage behavior, but you would be mistaken. This act while it may appear brutal or cruel has a purpose. The new leader of the pride understands that these bastard children do not share his genes or lineage and therefore will have no loyalty to him. The new lion understands that when they reach adulthood, they will be most likely to challenge his dominance. Finally, the new leader of the pride understands that these bastard cubs will be a drain on his resources. Male Lions comprehend there is no benefit in caring for another Lion's cubs and in many ways, it will ultimately be your doom. As human beings it would be unethical, immoral, and even criminal to follow the actions of the male Lion but the psychology behind it is priceless. Any man that is willing to get into relationship with a woman with children from another man is a loser.

The only exception being that a wife in a committed healthy relationship tragically or unexpectedly lost her husband.

However, we all know this scenario does not really exists in this modern era, so my original statement stands. A man that is willing to take care of another man's responsibilities is stating he is weak. This type of man does not think highly of himself and in many instances will display traits of low self-esteem. The man that is willing to enter a committed relationship with a woman who has children with other men is making a declaration. He is making the statement that he is not a man to be respected. Only men of lesser value entertain the idea of taking on the responsibilities of other men. In fact, the moment you accept a relationship on the terms and conditions of caring for another man's child your authority is essentially terminated. When a woman learns that a man is willing to take care of another man's child, she instantly labels him a beta-male. Certain YouTube creators and Authors will have you believe that if a man is willing to care for a family that does not belong to him women will praise you for stepping up. This could not be further from the truth. A woman views the man who is willing to take care of children she made with another man as less than human. She will assign him responsibilities and chores, but he will never be able to reap benefits.

I recall when I was younger and dating a female who lived with her stepfather. This man provided a house, ensured the bills were paid, and even provided the vehicles. He was a geek; he wore glasses and was very awkward in his mannerisms. I was in

Highschool and even at that time I understood why this man entered a relationship with this woman. This man believed that she was his better and he felt honored to be selected by her. She was a beautiful woman and she had beautiful daughters and this man was blinded by this fact. Beauty caused him to overlook glaring warning signs. He totally ignored the fact that while these children were beautiful, they were bastards. The man that helped to birth them also abandoned them. For whatever reason he did not think enough of them to remain a fixture in their lives in any capacity. The biological father was alive, but he did not participate in his daughters' lives. This man also did not marry her which is another red flag that should not have been overlooked. While he was the breadwinner in the household, he did not receive that type of respect from the mother or the daughters. They would laugh at him behind his back and make it clear to us that he was simply a resource. To them, his position was the designated bill payer nothing more. I remember he was in a heated disagreement with the two daughters. They disagreed about assigned chores. He made it clear that he paid the bills and expected the girls to do their part when one of the girls blurted out: "You are not my father!". Again, I was in Highschool, but I believe I had the intelligence to understand that these girls had more respect for the absent father than they did for the man who was there taking care of them. They displayed more appreciation for a man who did not think enough of them to remain, than the man who was raising them. They fearlessly raised their voices to him which clearly showed their lack of respect but there is a point that should not be overlooked.

The daughters were a clear representation of how the mother felt about the stepdad. If the mother respected him the daughters would have also. These two girls modeled the behavior of their mother towards him. She did not respect him, so they didn't feel the need to respect him either. The fact that this man was willing to take on another man's responsibility did not make him noble it made him desperate. This woman saw that desperation and she took advantage of that. She took his hospitality, his money, his care and concern and spit on him in the process. To make sure that he truly felt the sting of her disrespect she made sure her children from another man showed him disrespect as well. This is happening all over the country if not the world. Men are foolish enough to believe that if he willingly takes care of another man's child, he will get the admiration and respect of the women and the children. Unfortunately, this could not be further from the truth. A woman does not respect a man who is willing to take on another man's responsibility and with good reason. I do not blame a woman who takes advantage of a man who is willing to place himself in this situation. What this man is saying when he joins a ready-made family is that he is so pathetic, so desperate, so much of a loser that he is not worthy of a woman who has no baggage.

There are currently and estimated 7 billion people on the planet with 3.5 billion accounting for women. A man that selects a woman with children is stating he is such a coward he lacks the ability to attract a woman with no children. The man that joins a ready-made family is acknowledging that this woman has serious issues and he accepts her dysfunction. One of my favorite content creators (Blackram313) stated that the single mother is a terrible choice for a relationship because she inherently makes terrible decisions. The fact that she is a single mother is based on two possible reasons. The first is that she picked a man who has no father or husband qualities. Nothing about him stated he would be a good father or supportive mate. The second reason would be that she is so disagreeable, so disrespectful or combative that she forced the father of her children to abandon them. The importance of these two scenarios is that each of these selections only point to the fact she makes terrible decisions. What a single mother presents, is the fact that she is foolish enough to allow men to sleep with her without a commitment. She is not intelligent enough to require marriage to ensure that her children will be properly provided for. She also lacks the intelligence to take proper precautions to protect herself during sexual activity. As a man you must evaluate the logic of a single mother. This is a woman who is perfectly fine with allowing a man to have unprotected sex with her and recklessly produce a life. She requires no investment from this nameless, faceless man. For one night of passion she will condemn herself and her child to a life of poverty. If you disagree just look at the most recent United States Census Bureau statistics on single parent families. According to the statistic's single mothers account for 81% of single parent families. Of that number, single parent families living in poverty account for 35% in each individual state. You must understand the gravity of the statistics provided by the United States Census Bureau. Each of the 50 states has a single mother population that accounts for a minimum of 35% of the families living in poverty. Single mothers produce a great deal of the societal issues we face today. According to reports from the United States Census Bureau:

1) 63% of Suicides in the United States are from Single Parent Families
2) 90% of Homeless and Runaway Children
3) 85% of all children that exhibit behavior disorders
4) 80% of Rapist motivated with displaced anger (CDC)
5) 71% of All High School dropouts
6) 75% of Chemical Abuse Patients
7) 70% of Juveniles in state-operated institutions
8) 85% of all youths sitting in prisons

Based on the data single mothers are destroying the lives of their children and the society because they teach their children the art of dysfunction. It is no secret that a woman who has multiple bastards with multiple men are promiscuous. With this knowledge we must recognize that the single mother introduces a cycle of instability. In a child's lifetime he or she will most likely be introduced to many men who will come in and out of the picture. The child will attempt to make connections and they will abruptly end as these men will disappear without warning. This will be because the single mother is unable to pair bond and thus unable to maintain a stable relationship. Keep in mind she is a terrible judge of character so she will also be pumped and dumped by several bad boys as well. The single mother will continue to deliver confusion and chaos to her child/children through instability and poverty. The propaganda machine presents a false narrative about the sanctity of the single mother. They show you commercials of the strong woman who fearlessly braved through life to ensure her child grew into a respectable adult. You see films and hear stories about a woman being abandoned by some evil man and somehow having the courage to fight through the obstacles of life with her child/children. However, reality shows the statistical data and the evidence in relation to single mothers.

For the guys that are reading this book and thinking you are different because she gave you a child/children you are probably the biggest fool of them all. Men allow their egos to lead them into some very idiotic situations. Men believe if they can get the single mother to bare his children somehow, he has reset the clock. He is too stupid to acknowledge that most single mothers prefer this and not for the reason you may think. If a woman has bastard children and she can deceive a man into joining her dysfunctional family, her next move is to trap him by having his children. The first few children may have belonged to thugs, gangsters, or bad boys but eventually she is looking for a beta-male to complete her chaotic life. The beta-male does not understand that he is selected by the single mother because he has no alpha tendencies. While the previous men have knocked her up and abandoned her, your responsibility as the beta-male is to pick up the slack of the men before you. So, while she will have your child it is not really for you. The child is really her insurance policy to keep the beta-male in play. She may have four children and one of them may belong to the beta-male but by default he will take care of the other three children that do not belong to him. Single mothers are master manipulators so many men have foolishly fell for this trap. He believes she wants to have his child because she loves him and wants to have his children when she is really playing a numbers game. The beta-male is responsible and most likely educated. The beta-male most likely has a decent career with a pension and possibly an insurance policy. The fathers of her first children were most likely drug dealers, drug users, high school dropouts, criminals, etc. They have nothing to offer and she expects nothing from them. The beta-male however has everything to lose. The single mother understands that the beta-male's career is in jeopardy if he attempts to abandon her and he can even face imprisonment. Her goal is accomplished whether he stays with her or he leaves. Either the beta-male will stay with her and she will extract his resources, or he will leave, and she will extract his resources through child support.

A perfect example would be the marriage of a certain artist and athlete who will go unnamed. The Artist was a once successful pop/r&b artist who career abruptly ended in the early 2000's. She later connected with another artist who was becoming a big deal in the industry at that time. She quickly entered a relationship with him, and they had a child. Unfortunately for the artist she learned that he was not a man who could be easily controlled. He was his own man and lived by his own rules. Their relationship ended and she was a single mother. Of course, she would get child support, but she knew it would only last 18 years. She needed a beta-male to secure her future, enter the athlete. While he is a leader on the field, he has beta tendencies. This could not be more evident when he began his relationship with the artist. The father of her child is Alpha, so she did not require him to marry her. The father of her child brought that energy that attracts women. He was able to do whatever he wished to the artist and that includes get her pregnant. The athlete however is beta so he was required to marry the artist before he could impregnate her. The athlete is the "Good Guy" so his purpose is to provide. He does not arouse her sexually he is just a resource to be utilized for bills and care for her child with another man. Not only was the athlete required to marry this Single Mother, she sealed the deal with her pregnancy with the athlete's child. The Artist is not in love with the athlete nor does she Respect him. She is in love with his multi-million-dollar contract and what it brings her. The reason the artist does not respect the athlete is because she understands that with all his fame and fortune, he still lacks the confidence and self-respect to find himself a woman with a clean slate. The athlete has the money, looks, and career not only to find a beautiful woman in her late teens, early twenties but possibly a virgin with no children. Instead, he thought so low of himself he married and impregnated a single mother who slept with a number of men in her late 20's (Now 33). The Athlete is now trapped by his own beta-male behavior. He is a victim in this game, and he does not know it. It is my belief the artist will not stay with the athlete, based on the current behavior of the modern female, eventually she will leave. Why, because the artist does not respect the athlete and why should she? If he is foolish enough to join a ready-made family and take care of another man's child, he is a cuckold. The child she created with the athlete was the artist's insurance and she knew once she accomplished this he would have to care for her child with the other guy by default. To sum this chapter up, stay away from single mothers. They have nothing to offer you and they are seeking to trap you. A man that accepts a ready-made family is looking to be disrespected and punished. He is saying it is okay to use me as a utility and discard me when you're done. Any man that is willing to disregard his own linage, his ability to pass on his DNA to care for another guys children deserves what he gets. Don't be that guy.

Understanding The Concept Of Sexual Market Value

Women have always been rated based on their sexual market value, no exceptions. This system is like the stock exchange or a credit report and is designed to determine if she is an appreciating or depreciating asset. A woman's sexual market value is not something to be ignored. This concept determines if she will live a privileged life, a middle-class life, or be forced into a life of poverty. A woman's decisions at 18, 22, or 25 can have far reaching repercussions and be the starting point in a series of events that lead lifelong hardships. Many women are currently feeling the consequences of making poor decisions early regarding this subject because they failed to grasp the reality of the situation. It's like an athlete who received a multi-million contract and spent his career buying exotic cars, mansions, Yachts, taking women on expensive trips around the world etc. If you have seen the ESPN special titled "30 for 30 – Broke". Several athletes discuss how they wasted their money during their career and suddenly went into poverty. I saw a video in which a rapper walked into the middle of the street and proceeded to throw money in the air. The bills flew all over the street and many pedestrians began to retrieve the bills and place them in their pockets. The two situations I just described are obviously making terrible decisions that will revisit them in a manner they will not enjoy. This is like our discussion about women and sexual market value. They are wasting their assets on men and situations that yield no benefit and only decreases their value.

The first thing a woman must understand is that the assets a woman has are very valuable and can yield the greatest results between the ages of 18-25. This is the best time for a woman to utilize her womanly assets to attract the best male suitor to provide her with a comfortable and in some cases fairytale life. The ages of 18-25 yields a woman the power to accept and reject men as she sees fit. These ages are a display of her femininity and youthful appearance which is used as weapon to attract "Mr. Right". Unfortunately, women do not recognize their value and will squander it away investing in low value men and insignificant sexual experiences. Whether she cares to acknowledge this or not, a woman's value is determined by her sexual partners and experiences. Women despise the idea of being reduced to one part of their anatomy but that is because they do not appreciate the value it holds. In the stock market of life, the value of a woman is based on the number of men a woman has been with. If she is a virgin her value is extremely high. She will most likely select the best male suitor possible. If you don't believe that just ask the 20-year-old woman named jasmine who sold her virginity for $1,373,249.00 to a Wall Street Banker. The Wall Street Banker beat the other two offers of $1,073,880.00 and $715,462.00. While I do not condone this woman selling her virginity it is evidence of how significant this concept is. Jasmine was 22 years-old, pretty, and a virgin and all three of these things made her a millionaire in one night. She literally cashed in on her ability to remain a virgin well into her 20's.

This is evidence that in terms of sexual market value, virginity is the highest valued and most expensive stock. This does not mean if she is not a virgin, she will not be highly valued it just establishes this is the top level in the sexual market hierarchy. The fact of the matter is the less sexual partners a woman has experienced the higher her value in this stock exchange of life. If a woman has had two sexual partners in her lifetime, she will be far more desired than a woman who has been with 10 or 15 men. Many women have failed to grasp this concept and have instead embraced the teachings of feminism. Feminism has taught women they can have as many sexual partners as they wish and call it freedom. Unfortunately, what they are doing is destroying their sexual market value and any hope of a meaningful future with an ideal partner. I'm pretty sure at this point I am being labeled as sexist or old fashioned by women who are reading this, but we cannot deny truth. Look at articles like "Millennials are having less sex than any other generation" in the L.A. Times. Also be sure to read "Americans are not having sex, according to national survey" in the Washington Post. There are thousands of articles on this subject and you can find them all over the internet. There are many reasons people site for this new phenomenon and they seek to shame men for this situation. They love to say things like guys are still living at home with their parents or men are afraid to commit. While this does account for a certain percentage, this is a false representation of the problem. The reality of the matter is the sexual market value of the modern-day woman is in the deep negative. With the emergence of the feminist ideology the sexual stock market has plummeted and is currently in a recession. Women have no value or currency to trade. As women have pursued education, employment, sexual freedom, drinking and drugs they have destroyed any chance at marriage, relationships, or a traditional home life. Some women will say they don't want the traditional life. They don't want the husband, the children, or dog and if that is the case it still will not account for the breakdown in modern day relationships. What has occurred is the modern woman has proven to be a risky investment with no reward.

In this current environment, and as harsh as it may seem, most modern women have no value. The reason the male population has overwhelmingly adopted this position is because women have rejected the qualities that attract men while they embraced the feminist ideology. This ideology has taught women to abandon the sexual market value model and feel comfortable with engaging in sexual encounters freely. Women have been taught that sleeping with many men is empowerment and failed to present the consequences. The film industry, Television, music, and Social Media use propaganda to encourage women to abandon marriage, relationships, and family. The social programming has been successful. Modern society has taught women that they do not need to have morals, ethics, or self-respect. They can wear outlandish clothing, ridiculous weaves, display the most ignorant behavior and they will be rewarded with money and male suitors. What feminist and women fail to do is anticipate the future. I did a video on my YouTube channel "Male Enlightenment TV" titled "Top 4 Ways Your Diet Is Linked To Your Relationships". In this video I explained how relationships are like a trip to the supermarket. I stated in the supermarket of life we should be in the produce section selecting fruits and vegetables because they are healthy. However, many of us end up in the isle with the soda, chips, cookies, and cakes. We do this because this food is quick and taste good however overtime junk food has dangerous and deadly effects. Prolonged consumption of junk food and fast food can lead to diabetes, heart disease, high blood pressure, stroke and other serious health issues. It is at that moment when the doctor tells you have Cancer that you start to think about the produce section. You begin to think "I should have maintained a better diet". The same is true in relationships.

Women chase after the "Bad Boy" or the "Alpha Male" because they are the fast food of men. They seem exciting and it appears that they are more fun. However, women who have prolonged exposure to these men find they will most certainly be labeled and have very little to no chance of becoming a fiancé/wife. A woman that chooses to exercise her right to sleep with a great deal of men is only investing in loneliness. She is sentencing herself to the friends with benefits, side chick, or hook up realm. Promiscuous women have no sexual market value and ultimately have nothing to trade. Men are not intimidated by women who have slept with many men they simply do not have any use for them. Sure, they will have sex with you but nothing more. Prepare to be called during late evening hours when he needs to get off. However, you will never be invited to family gatherings, or holiday events. You are a dirty little secret with the emphasis on dirty. Many modern-day women have failed to assess the situation properly or even think about their future in terms of the sexual market value exchange and they are suffering for it. More women are alone today than ever before because they failed to think about the consequences of sexual promiscuity. In their old age no one is willing to invest. Who wants a 35 to 40-year-old woman who has slept with over 30 men and has bastard children? These types of women are only considered for sex.

According to the sexual market value exchange a woman in her late 20's and 30's has very little to no value for a man seeking to build a family. It's like when rappers buy very expensive vehicles. They buy a $450,000.00 dollar Bentley and proceed to modify it. They place video game systems, televisions, rims, and have their name stitched in the leather. They smoke weed and drink in the vehicle. Finally, when they wish to sell it, they find out the Bentley dealerships will purchase that $450,000.00 dollar vehicle for less than $100,000.00. This occurs because the more you move the vehicle from its natural state the more it loses its value. People who can afford these expensive vehicles do not wish to purchase one that has chrome rims, Tv's in the headrest, someone's name stitched in the interior or videogame systems. They want the factory design and specifications because that is what ensures the vehicle will perform to the highest quality and maintain its beauty. The same is true when we discuss women. Men marry women who are virgins or very close to it. Men are interested in women who have self-respect, morals and ethics. They want women who dress appropriately and know they do not have to dress like a harlot for a man's attention. They understand that wild color hair, bull piercings, face piercings, tattoos, excessive make-up etc. takes away from their beauty. They understand that all these things take away from a woman's value and makes her less desirable. The modern woman has adopted the behaviors of a harlot and believe they should be valued as a mother and a wife.

The modern woman views men as the "Patriarchy" not realizing the regulated sexual marketplace was created for their benefit. They do not realize that many years ago men knew the value of women and the dangers of not protecting them from other men and themselves. The strict emphasis on virginity and chastity was designed to ensure the honor of the woman and her family. As I said previously, a woman's sexual history determined her station in life. Virgins held the highest probability for a financially comfortable and stable life while promiscuous women were certainly guaranteed to die penniless in a gutter. The propaganda machine is hard at work seeking to rewire the thought process of men because they understand that our value system is based on this fundamental fact. Men love to watch and sleep with porn stars, strippers, prostitutes, and thots but no man wants to marry them.   These types of women do not get the house, cars, credit cards or bank accounts no matter how Hollywood attempts to make you think otherwise. Do not get your validation from reality tv just go outside and look at your world. How many of your female friends and family members are married? How many of your female co-workers are married? Are you married? In most cases the answer is no because men have abandoned this stock, they know it is worthless. An article by Mark Regnerus titled "Cheap Sex and the Decline of Marriage" for the Wall street Journal spoke on this. The Author explained For American men, sex has become rather cheap. As compared to the past, many women expect little in return for sex, in terms of time, attention, commitment or fidelity. Men, in turn do not feel compelled to supply these goods as they once did. The author is explaining as more women began to embrace feminism and have sex with a high volume of men, suddenly they became worthless. If you think of it in terms of the I Phone or the Samsung Galaxy, the regulated sexual marketplace operated in the same manner. When these companies release a new phone, they create demand by keeping supplies low. When this happens, you see the demand for this product increase. People are willing to pay far above the MSRP to have them. However, if the market were flooded with these phones people would not be interested. The same is true for the current state of the dating scene. In the past women ensured that access to sex scarce and this made it more valuable. Men were willing to invest in this commodity because it was not readily available. Men were willing to give Marriage, Financial Security, a home, vehicles and access to the bank accounts and credit cards for regular access to women. However, in recent times this market has been flooded with easy access to sex. Thanks to the feminist ideology, women believe giving their bodies away to many men is somehow liberation. They believe being able to say they slept 20, 30, 40 men is somehow a badge of honor. The modern woman has been taught to freely engage in sexual activity with a high volume of men while complaining about patriarchy. This is the equivalent of a company having a highly desired product and instead of capitalizing on it they give it away for free while insulting the customers. The other reality we must recognize is that the woman who has been promiscuous is essentially dead inside. She has no feelings and no emotions. She is unable to pair bond or build meaningful relationships with the opposite sex. She is unable to respect men and this is mostly because she does not respect herself. She lost that ability years ago. She doesn't even enjoy sex it's just something to do. It is a way to fight off boredom or loneliness. Based on this new reality men have abandoned traditional relationships while the sexual marketplace has fell into a recession and soon a depression.

Yes, Your Own Mother Is An Accomplice

When I was younger, I dated a young lady while simultaneously receiving an education in relationship politics. My father provided some lessons but unfortunately, he failed to go into detail. His information was very vague, and it forced me to learn many of my lessons through experience. However, I do recall with this young lady I did present an Alpha Male demeanor with no difficulty. It was as if this behavior was built into my genetics. I recall an evening in which we were talking on the telephone because back then most couples spoke on the landline for hours. This evening one of my friends came to visit and wanted me to go out with him. I had spoken with my girlfriend for a few hours that evening and thought nothing of ending our conversation and joining my friend.

"So, listen Mike is here so I'm going to let you go and speak to you tomorrow" I stated.

"Are you telling me or are you asking me?" My girlfriend asked.

"I don't have to ..." I tried to finish.

I was about to let my girlfriend know I didn't need her permission until my mother intervened. My mother asked me to place the call on hold which I did. She explained what I did was wrong.

"You should have asked her if it was okay for you to go out with your friend" My mother stated.

I was confused, I really didn't have any life experience or anything I was a teenager. However, what my mother was saying to me did not feel right. To be honest it felt stupid and I didn't want to do it.

"Why do I have to ask her permission?" I asked confused.

"Because she needs to know that you consider her when you make decisions"

Again, I did not feel comfortable with this, but my girlfriend is on the line and my mother is in my face and they are both shaming me for not asking for permission to hang with a friend. Like most men I just gave in.

"Vanessa is it okay if I go hang out for a little bit with Mike?" I asked defeated.

"Yes, you can, I will talk to you tomorrow" She finished victorious.

Whenever I revisit this interaction in my mind it brings feelings of regret and anger. In many ways this was the defining moment that began the mental cold war between myself and my mother. This was not a moment of appropriate etiquette this was beta-male training 101. My mother was seeking to suppress my alpha energy and reprogram my thoughts with beta responses. This interaction was a form of submission and my girlfriend at the time as well as my mother were working as a team to implement the beta initiative. It was something about the entire interaction that did not sit right with me and over the years situations along these lines would continuously occur. I can recall when I had issues in my relationships I would look to my mother for advice and receive a completely unexpected outcome. My mother would say things like "Well... what did you do to make her respond that way" or "Here's what you did wrong". It appeared that I was to blame for all conflict in my relationships. It was not until I reached adulthood that I understood what had occurred. My mother was seeking to convert me into a beta-male. It is hard to believe that the woman who gave birth to me has worked to ensure that I walk onto a plantation and slave away for the glory of some woman who would most likely extract my resources and divorce rape me.

I do not want to confuse anyone; I am sure my mother loves me with all her heart. She carried me for nine months so we have a connection that can never be broken. However, as I made the transition to a young adult my mother's allegiance shifted to the sisterhood. My mother's obligations lie with the success of women and in this war, I am the enemy. As men we only see our mother. She is the person who fed us, kissed our bobo's, and guided us through childhood. Unfortunately, we all forgot above all, she is a woman first. Believe it or not your mother's primary function is the empowerment of women even if that means you suffer in the process. We have been programmed by society to believe women are made of sugar, spice, and everything nice. We have been told that if we treat them nice and bring them gifts, they would love us and appreciate what we do for them. Nothing could be further from the truth. Through experience and observation, we have learned that women do not respect any of this. The men who treat woman like garbage and do not care about their feelings carry their favor. The man that does not acknowledge their presence will gain all their attention. Many men had to learn this through experience because it is a trade secret that your mother will never reveal to you. She will never tell you that in order to keep a woman you have to provide chaos and instability. You must be unpredictable and erratic. She will never tell you that you must come home one day and be very loving and then the following day you must flip items over and yell. Your mother will never tell you that the best thing to do in a relationship is let your woman see that other women want you. Your mother will never tell you that being an asshole is the best thing you can do.

The question of course being, why wouldn't your mother tell you these things? She could have saved you a lifetime of misery and pain if she sat you down and told you about female nature. Your mother could have given you insider information you needed to navigate relationships. Instead, she has watched you try and fail multiple times with no intention of giving you the keys to the kingdom. The reason for this is your mother is a lifetime card carrying member of the sisterhood and you as a man are considered cattle. What happens in these situations is women access their prior relationships and apply them to your situations. I have had numerous conversations with my mother about the Modern woman and the immoral and unethical behaviors they engage in. I explain how the women of the past were far more respectful of themselves, their families, and society. However, my mother still finds a way to become offended about my criticisms of the modern woman. This happens because women identify with one another, so an attack of this generation is somehow an attack on all women past and present. Her goal is to train me to be a beta-male and lead a life of servitude on the gynocentric plantation. I realize this because she is not concerned about how I feel about relationships. After my last relationship ended, I knew I would never invest in women again. I knew I would never get married, have a steady girlfriend, move a woman in my home, or move into a woman's home. At that moment I knew that I would only deal with women in terms of friends with benefits and more importantly on my terms.

Despite my protest and objections to relationships, my mother would totally ignore my feelings on the matter and say, "You just picked the wrong one this time, but you will find the right one". My mother does not care that all my negative life experiences are connected to seeking to please a woman in a relationship. Now that I recognized marriage and relationships are of no benefit to me, she is working hard to lead me back to the plantation. My mother will say things like "Well in your next relationship you will be wiser". However, I understand she is saying this because she is seeking to subliminally plant the seed that will encourage me back to the plantation. A statement like this implies that I should be looking to get back in a relationship despite this being the furthest thing from my mind. However, it is not important what I want, it seems there are never enough beta-males in society and the recruitment of fresh souls is mandatory. Across this country mothers are indoctrinating their sons into this system of servitude knowing they are dooming them to a lifetime of failure. Mothers are turning their sons into the very man they do not want to be with. They are using the male child's developmental years to remove his alpha tendencies. You see this in education as well. Boys love to wrestle and play because they are building their alpha tendencies. They understand competition amongst men builds confidence, courage, as well as other manly traits. However, this behavior is discouraged in school. It is a key component to the development of men and yet it is dismissed as horseplay. An online website title "The American Interest" wrote an article titled "Boys punished for being boys" In this article they ask, are boys being punished for exhibiting trait characteristics of their gender?

The answer to this question is yes and everyone is in on the conspiracy including your mother. Just like the education system it seems that mothers across the country are hard at work ensuring that their sons prepare for a life on the plantation and relationship slavery. The tragedy is that our mothers are seeking to turn us in to men they do not respect and do not want to be with. These women are attracted to men who live outside of relationship rules. They are passionate about men who reject the plantation and conformity. The beta-male is the consolation prize for a used up promiscuous woman that alpha men no longer want. As Chris Rock stated when it comes to the beta-male "You were not her first choice". Based on this fact many unsuspecting men are fooled into relationships and marriages. They learn the harsh truth they were not her first choice. Men are losing their homes, investments, property, and children because they made the mistake of accepting the beta-male programming. Despite this crisis our mothers are not sitting us down and explaining the true nature of the opposite sex, instead they are sending their sons into the symbolic slaughterhouse. Our mothers have raised us to believe we should take these women out to dinner, buy them gifts for Valentine's Day, Anniversaries, and holidays. Our mothers have taught us that we must be submissive and bend the knee to our female overlords. She has trained us to believe that women can do no wrong so by default we are always in violation. If she is without blame as your mother has taught you then you are to blame. All men have been groomed to believe this and very few of us escape the programming. We allow the lessons of our mothers to lead us into marriages with women who do not love us. We allow these lies that have been taught to us to rule our lives and consume us over and over. It all begins at home with our mothers who begin the process of manipulation early. They may use guilt or shaming to get you to do their bidding.

I remember when I was younger my father was always the bad guy in all family disagreements. I will not say that he was innocent or that he should not be assigned blame. However, if you ask my mother, my father was over 100% responsible for all the difficulties in her life. She had even trained me and my brother to believe this as well. She would tell us stories about how he pursued her and was persistent like it was not her decision to be with him. If you listen to her stories, she never had a choice in the matter. My mother led us to believe that my father was a monster whose sole purpose was to make her miserable. However, she was always innocent in all these stories. This was social programming on the part of my mother to get us to identify not only my father but men as the villain. This conditioning was designed to teach us to be different towards women. We were meant to learn to treat them better but, it was making us weak. While I love my mother with all my heart, I understand that she is a woman first and an accomplice to female behavior. With this information gentlemen we must understand that she must be treated as an informant and enemy combat in matters of relationships and women. Many times, the information our mothers give us about relationships is tainted information based on her desire to manipulate your father. I know it is difficult to believe but yes, your mother is an accomplice to female behavior.

Why The Concept Of Love Is Not Real
Love Vs. Respect

I remember an episode of "Mad Men" where the main character Don Draper was talking to a woman that he wanted to sleep with. She also wanted to sleep with him, but she wanted a relationship as well. I believe she was attempting to use the promise of sex to get him to leave his wife. Of course, Don Draper was an alpha, so her attempt was in vain but the monologue that followed placed everything in perspective for me. They were discussing why she was not married. The woman stated she loves the thrill of business and she has never been in love to which Draper responded:

"She won't get married because she's never been in love... I think I wrote that just to sell nylons" He finished.

"For a lot of people love isn't just a slogan" she responded.

"Oh, you mean love, you mean a big lightning bolt to the heart where you can't eat and you can't work and you just run off and get married and make babies... The reason you have not felt it, is because it doesn't exist. What you call love was invented by guys like me, to sell nylons" He finished.

It was an epiphany realized, a mental awakening. It was a true understanding that everything that I had ever done regarding relationships and everything I had ever believed about them was a lie. The blue pill mindset that was given to me by the education system, Hollywood, corporations, and even my parents had set me up for a 100% failure rate in relationships. Think about your earliest memories on the playground and the social politics that surrounded your interaction with girls. Most little boys were fearless demonstrating alpha tendencies. All we wanted to do was play and be active. Your earliest memories were of competition and sport. At this time in your life girls held no special influence and could not control the minds of little boys. She could not use the promise of a kiss because the boys were not interested. Many "Do You Like Me?" notes went unanswered because we were playing cops and robbers or tag. In fact, many little girls were unwilling practice dummies for wrestling moves little boys wanted to test out. In fact, I am sure you can recall when you were younger some girls you may have ruffed up who went off crying and screaming only to return minutes later for more punishment. At these ages we were not exposed to social programming and propaganda that policed our behavior with girls, so your default setting was alpha. However, this would change when adults would intervein. Teachers, parents, other authority would scold and chastise you about how you are supposed to treat girls. They told you to be nice to them, they are sensitive and delicate. Suddenly, you had a new set of rules to follow where society expected you to place them above you. The establishment sent you subliminal messages that you are required to chase her, court her, taker her on dates, buy her gifts, finally get down on one knee and beg her to be yours forever.

We were being reprogrammed by a system that wanted us to worship the gynocracy and place them first. One of the first things they taught us to ensure our path to destruction was the word and the concept of love. We are not talking about the love you feel for your family and friends or pets. We are talking about the concept of love we have been indoctrinated to believe is real when dealing with romantic relationships. As men we have been told to submit to an emotion that is irrational and abandon our logic. We have been taught to operate based on feelings and this has destroyed our ability to maintain a relationship. All around us we have been bombarded with a propaganda campaign that weakens our ability to utilize independent thought. Corporations have taught us we must participate in the charade of "Love". If not our girlfriends and wives will turn against us and utilize shaming language, ridicule, and other forms of coercion. We blindly follow an invisible and fabricated emotion based on what many people believe is insanity.

Love is an emotion and concept that teaches dependence, encourages infatuation, and servitude. Men are required to submit to a woman by expressing what he believes is "love" and constantly renew "loyalty" by providing gifts and resources. Participating in this ritual is not natural for men because it physically and emotionally removes his masculinity and ensures that he remains a blue-pill beta in the service of women. Love encourages men to perform insane acts based on irrational behavior with no regard for its consequences. Love will encourage and in many cases force men to provide gifts and trinkets that they are unable to afford. This act will ultimately lead many men to financial ruin. Men have fallen into deep financial debt providing a woman with a lifestyle he is unable to afford. Men have purchased homes and vehicles that they could not afford as an expression of love. Men have spent hundreds of thousands of dollars on dates, clothing, jewelry, travel, bills, holidays, vacations and other expenses because they were taught this is how you express love. We did not realize that we were being miseducated by a system that required our slavery in order to operate. We did not realize that providing these gifts and resources were a display of our weakness and would be used against us. If you are observant you will notice that a woman will never stop a man from purchasing expensive or life changing items for her. This is because the moment you do, she knows that you are her slave. She does appreciate what you provide because she does not respect you. The word love is her weapon that she will use against you to get cash and prizes while ensuring you continue to be her slave. Love is a manipulation word designed to keep you focused on the idea that she is the most important thing in your world. You must continue to prove that daily or for as long as she will have you. Love is submission, it is the tacit agreement that she controls you and it is also the reason that every single relationship you have ever had has failed. The fact you went into a relationship or marriage based on Love sent her the message that she is your master and you are her slave. A woman that does not respect you wants you to spend money and a woman that respects you wants to help you increase your wealth.

I recall a time in my past when I was talking with a woman who was dating and preparing for marriage. She had the idea in her head that her wedding was going to be at least $20,000 dollars. I asked her "You don't think that money would be better utilized buying a house?". She lived in a small apartment and after the wedding she was going to return to that small apartment. She did not care the guy stupid enough to marry her would start off $20,000 dollars in debt because she did not plan on being with him anyway. He would just be a means to an end. Her real goal was to find a man stupid enough to fall in love with her. She would manipulate him into going in debt for the purpose of having a glorious wedding. Even when she decided to end the relationship, he would still have to make payments on the marriage after the divorce. Women understand that the word love is a made-up word and the person that feels that emotion is the loser.

She uses the word love to control you like the puppeteer parasite or the zombie parasite. Just like these parasites that control the minds and bodies of their infected host you are experiencing something similar with the idea of love. Buying that expensive home, expensive vehicle, jewelry, clothes, trips, access to bank accounts and credit cards is all a form of control. She uses that word love to invade and infect your mind and prevent any rational thought. It only after she has left that the spell wares off and you realize you were being controlled. It is only when you find yourself paying divorce attorneys, child support and alimony that you realize the parasite injected you with the chemical agent love and has nearly if not successfully bankrupted you. It Is only when you see that she has more respect for some guy that has done nothing for her that you realize how much your love was worth. She wants you to continuously tell her that you love her because if you continue this process, she knows that you are still under her spell. We have all failed in our previous relationships because we were indoctrinated into the blue-pill beta mindset. We were taught to believe in a fabricated emotion based on a manufactured mentality that encourages obedience to the gynocracy. Those of us who fail to recognize what has taken place are doomed to repeat the same process because we have no knowledge of the fact that, we are in a relationship matrix. The fact you accepted this concept of love has made you weak and she has taken advantage of your ignorance and used it against you. If you do not believe that just look at the United States Census data that confirms divorce rates have skyrocketed since the 1980's and hit all new highs in the 2000's. Women account for more than 80% of all divorces filed in the United States. If this fabricated emotion of love were real, why would it be so easy for women to abandon their husband and separate the family to the tune of 80%? It is because they know what many of us as men have failed to understand, love is a fallacy. It is a beautiful word to describe your slavery and the reality that your mind has been invaded by a parasite. What you perceive as love is simply infatuation mixed with co-dependency and desperation. As men it is time for us to unlearn this harmful concept and walk away from the mental and physical plantation that government, corporations, Hollywood, Music, Family, and Women have burdened us with.

So, some may ask "If we are not supposed to love them how do we build relationships with them?" The answer is simple, it is what we should have based all our relationships on and the lack of it is the reason many of us have found the red pill. All our relationships with women should have been based on RESPECT. From the beginning she should have been placed in a position where she had to earn your respect. She should have been forced to prove she was worthy of your time. If she is placed in a position in which she must earn your respect she is required to demonstrate value. She is required to show what she can contribute to your life and what benefits she can provide. In her quest to earn your respect she must show evidence that she can add to your bottom line. She must prove she can be an appreciating asset. When you eliminate love from your vocabulary and base your relationship on respect your letting her know you are immune to the hypnotic song of her parasitic nature and cannot be influenced. When you base your relationship on respect you are asking her to produce evidence that she is invested and a contributing member in this relationship. A woman that is seeking to demonstrate value is not looking to extract your resources she is looking to help you increase them and build a stronger foundation. Placing a woman in a position where she must earn your respect eliminates her hypergamous nature. A man in love wants to do everything he can to keep that woman from leaving. However, a man that has based his relationship on respect does not care if she leaves. A man who has based his relationship on demanding that she earns his respect is completely aware of his value and does not allow anyone to distract from this fact. Forcing a woman to earn your respect eliminates the sense of entitlement, the narcissistic behavior, and the urge to act on hypergamy. However, if she is not interested in earning your respect you have lost nothing because this method prevents you from fully investing. As more men have started taking the red pill many post wall, promiscuous, predatory, single mothers have grown furious with the changing landscape of dating. Their once plentiful hunting ground littered with unsuspecting blue-pilled betas is now slowly becoming a barren waste land based on this understanding. Now that men are fully aware that love is concept forced on us by our corporate overlords to sell jewelry, wedding packages, and Valentine's Day Candy we see the fallacy in the word. If a woman ever attempts to use the word love on you, she is looking to mentally gain control of you, but the truly enlightened man knows she must earn your respect.

The Modern Woman Is Dead Inside

I was listening to a content creator who invited a woman to discuss relationships and if promiscuity was a major factor in the breakdown of dating and marriage. They discussed various real-life situations that ended based on the woman's need to be "Sexually Free" or "Find Herself". As you would expect, a woman's need to be unfaithful, abandon a relationship, marriage, or separate the family is exclusively the man's fault. The guest on the show explained that the man must have done something to cause this woman to be unfaithful, abandon the marriage, and separate this man from his children. The guest continued her rant solely placing responsibility on the man saying something to the effect of he must be horrible in bed. As the episode continued, she became more comfortable and began discussing her sexual exploits. She explained that she had a group of men that she sleeps with regularly. She discussed episodes in which she solicited men for sex and what types of penises she prefers. The woman talked about how she held no inhibitions sleeping with men she thought were attractive. The guest freely discussed specific encounters. The woman revealed that she had slept with more than twenty men. The woman finally ended her segment because she needed to "Get A Blunt" or smoke marijuana for those who may not know the language.

It was at that moment I realized; the modern woman is dead inside. She has lost her soul to dysfunction, chaos, and confusion. She worships at the altar of feminism and prays to the gods of sexual promiscuity, abortion, body mutilation and disease. The modern woman is a vapid void of insanity that seeks to drain the light and energy of anyone who is foolish enough to enter her orbit. The modern woman has abandoned her morals, values, ethics, and decency. She is no longer a respectable individual worthy of courtship and marriage. The modern woman is a whore who fucks for money, narcissism, and revenge. She has selfishly destroyed the dating market, the sanctity of marriage, and the nuclear family. The modern woman has happily become a prostitute that sells her body and her soul. Listening to that guest on that content creators livestream opened my eyes to the reality that he was not talking to a woman or a lady of any kind. This content creator was talking to a zombie whose body had withered away long ago. This female has slept with many men and its effects had taken its toll. She no longer saw sex as something that was sacred or that it should be experienced between two people who cared about one another. To this woman, it was just something to do. This is a major character flaw in the modern-day female because it is a clear indicator that she is a narcissist and sociopath. The way this guest presented herself was evidence that the men she had been with were simply a blur with no meaning. When a woman is dead inside, she no longer appreciates beauty she lives and thrives in a world of chaos. Her energy is misery, and confusion.

As men, we fail to recognize the reality that the women we are interested are a shell their former self and expired many years ago. We think that if we love her, she will change her ways. To our horror we discover that you can never resurrect the dead. We get ourselves involved in unhealthy relationships with women who are clearly damaged from previous experiences. They are no longer able to make meaningful connections. A woman that is dead inside is excited by all the things we consider unethical, immoral, and just wrong. She enjoys sleeping with men who are criminals, losers, delinquents, violent, and abusive. She derives pleasure from the pain of dealing with these types of men. The fact she no longer has any light inside helps her to embrace the darkness in her soul. This type of woman will engage in a twisted relationship with the worst type of men because the dysfunctional behavior they bring makes her feel something. This is her sick attempt at feeling alive. When she is mentally and physically abused, mistreated, and discarded the emotional rollercoaster gives her the illusion that she still walks among the living. The reason she is repulsed by the educated men or men with self-respect is because this type of man reminds her that she is dead inside. A man with self-respect only reinforces the reality that she is damaged and is unable to function in his world. The woman that is dead inside is operating on her most primitive instincts. Like a feral beast she gives into immediate gratification instead of taking the time to appreciate the long-term consequences. The woman that is dead inside has many sexual partners to fill the empty void. She fails to understand that she is increasing her misery with every sexual encounter. The more she attempts to hide the truth she is dead emotionally, the more it reveals itself.

All over social media you will see clear examples of women who are dead inside and the behaviors that reveal they are on a crash course to self-destruction. For Example, the woman who chants "My Body My Choice" wants you to believe that she is fighting for the right to decide about her anatomy. She wants you to believe this is a moral crusade based on legal and political freedom. However, she is fighting for the right to be a whore and kill babies. Only a woman who is dead inside would brag and boast about her ability to kill her unborn children. Only a woman who is no longer living would display her irresponsibility for the world to see, especially when there are so many preventative measures available to her. When she lashes out in anger at laws that reduce her ability to kill her children it is not because she seeks freedom from draconian laws and men trying to control her body. It is because she is being held accountable for her actions. She wants to fuck the guy she met on social media with no protection. Despite the very high probability of creating a child, she wants the option to erase her reckless behavior by going to an abortion clinic. The woman that is dead inside has no morals or values so if killing unborn children helps her avoid responsibility this is what will happen. In the African American community alone The United States Government with the Assistance of Margaret Sanger has ensured more than 30 million murders of unborn children. Apart from harm to the parent, rape, or serious birth complications the woman that uses abortion clinics as birth control is a twisted individual. Only a sociopath would engage in this behavior.

Women who are dead inside celebrate being a whore. She views her sexual deviant behavior as an accomplishment. This type of woman is so damaged she engages in extremely dangerous sexual activity that will most likely have serious health consequences. She engages in dangerous sexual activities hoping to feel something because she can no longer derive pleasure from the simple things. She has experienced a metaphorical death and needs to participate in sensation seeking activity to experience some form of happiness. Like a drug addict she has sex with a vast number of men hoping to relive her first high or sexual encounter. Each night she allows nameless faceless men to have her only to face reality and disappointment in the morning. Each time she has sexual contact she quickly learns that the experience did not provide comfort, so she dies a little more inside. However, the woman who is dead inside rationalizes her self-destructive behavior as exploring and gaining new experiences. She brags and boast about her sexual exploits with a multitude of men as if she is victorious in the experience. She tells you about the many different men that she has slept with as if it is a notch on her belt of conquest. This is the backward thinking of a dysfunctional damaged individual. Think about this concept in the terms of the person living in poverty. Based on the reality a person is financially deprived; many spend their lives seeking to convince others they are not living in poverty. They buy expensive clothing, jewelry, shoes, cars and speak very loudly about their ability to purchase items. This is a diversionary tactic designed to hide the obvious. The irony is, the more they spend to convince you they are not living in poverty the more they throw themselves into deeper financial ruin. The Same is true of the promiscuous woman and her behaviors. She is psychologically damaged by the reality that she has allowed several men to use her as a sexual object, so she attempts to turn the idea on its head. Instead of looking at the situation in terms of her reputation, mental state, and body are being compromised with all this meaningless sexual activity. She claims this destructive behavior as her strength.   The woman on the content creators show was speaking about her many sexual exploits as if she were the master of her sexual destiny. Many women in her situation attempt to change the narrative. Feminism is guilty of helping women indulge in this self-destructive behavior. Instead of teaching women to value themselves and treat the act of sex as something sacred, they helped to create generations of whores who give themselves away to anyone at any opportunity. As I previously stated, a woman's body was once a very high valued currency. She had the ability to gain wealth and security based on her selection of a husband. The unspoken deal was that she would remain a virgin and the man would provide her with a comfortable life in exchange. However, in modern times the female has shattered that concept. She believes she can sleep with anyone she wants whenever she chooses.   She then has the audacity to believe that her used up body should continue to be viewed as valuable. The woman that is dead inside believes that she should be able to engage in reckless sexual behavior and still have access to high value men. Her justification for such behavior is that men do it all the time but what she continues to conveniently ignore is that she is not a man.

Another sign that a woman is dead inside is her constant need to use drugs and/or alcohol. She has participated in threesomes, gangbangs, bukkake's, and attempts to justify her behavior as taking control of her sexuality. However, the more she engages in these types of behaviors the more she loses herself. The more she is faced with the reality of guilt and depression. She must resort to measure that will allow her to forget her transgressions. Therefore, most promiscuous women drink, smoke marijuana, as well as other drugs and medications. The drugs are a convenient excuse and lowers her sober inhibitions. Drugs and alcohol provide her with false courage and the ability to evade accountability. Many times, when a woman has been exposed for immoral sexual behavior her automatic excuse is usually "I was drunk", "I had too much to drink" or some variation of that statement. This is the method she uses to remove any responsibility, but it is also a way to cope with her shame. A woman that allows herself to be placed in compromising positions with men constantly relives the events in her mind. Each time she plays the event back in her head she feels the shame and embarrassment in real time. For this reason, she hates being sober and turns to drugs and alcohol just to be able to deal with herself. Therefore, you see several promiscuous women with alcohol, drugs or even medication on social media, photos, or her everyday life. The woman that is dead inside presents drug use as a part of the "Party till You Drop" life. She wants you to think that this is part of having fun but, she is trying to forget that she was involved in a gangbang last night. She wants to forget that she was being passed around last week. She wants to forget all those one-night stands from the dating sites and being intoxicated or high helps her accomplish this.

Another way you can identify a woman that is dead inside is by her self-mutilation and desecration of her own body. Women who are dead inside participate in the practice because the pain and the scares are a way to feel something. While dangerous sexual encounters are the leading method, they use to satisfy their desire for sensation seeking, Tattoos and piercing are the next best substitute. The more absurd or ridiculous the tattoos or piercings, the more pain they are looking to hide. The more outrageous the display the more pain they are experiencing. Woman who are dead inside usually attempt to cover their bodies in tattoos and piercings as way to attract attention because they feel invisible. It is usually a desperate and self-destructive attempt to stand out and be recognized. She feels dead inside, empty, a shell of what was once there so the best way to compensate in her mind is to do something drastic that will constantly demand attention. The promiscuous woman believes that people look at her in admiration or at least that is what her delusional state suggest. However, what men and women alike actually see is a whore, and person with low value, an individual with little respect for herself or others. The extreme piercings and tattoos scream "I am easy" or some variation of it. The piercings and tattoos are identifying marks of an individual that is damaged and unstable in several ways. The items especially in excess tell the story of someone who is traumatized by past events or damaged by immoral behavior. Her flashy tattoos and shiny piercings are a warning sign of danger if you attempt to engage with a woman who is dead inside.

The woman that is dead inside is also known for her gross misuse of make-up. She uses extreme make-up applications to distract from the reality of her excessive sexual activity, abortions, drinking & drugs, as well as tattoos and piercings are taking a toll on the body. The woman that is dead inside learns the hard way that all these activities steal your youth, beauty, and health which are all the weapons a woman needs to attract a man. Without here youth, beauty, or health she has no power and will be relegated to the shadows of society. The woman that is dead inside understands that her ability to attract men is necessary to ensure her access to a better life so she desperately turns to make-up to cover the years of damage she has done to her face. The woman that is dead inside attempts to conceal her transgressions with massive amounts of make-up. She hopes that men are unable to see the years of damage and abuse not realizing the make-up reveals far more than she could have imagined. The more make-up a woman wears the more men realize that she has terrible secrets she is trying to hide. Many women are beginning to resemble drag queens which reveals a great deal about where they have been and what they have done. Excessive make-up is a woman's acknowledgement that she has caused so much damage to her appearance she must use these chemicals to hide her shame from would be suitors. The fact that she is willing to subject herself to this daily routine is evidence that she has a great deal of skeletons she wishes to keep concealed. This type of woman wears her mask as a daily ritual which is also in many ways a reminder of who she really is and where she has been. For men who are unable to identify the woman that is dead inside they can become distracted and even infatuated with what they perceive as beauty only to later discover that this is a complete falsehood. Many men have learned the hard way that they have fallen in love with a fantasy, and her reality is a sobering experience. Without the make-up you see the crow's feet, the skin damage, the loss of youth, the blemishes, the scares, and the pimples. You see a woman who spent years disrespecting herself and destroying her body and her face reveals this fact. She spends and eternity trying to hide from reality, but the make-up can only temporarily hide your truth. She is dead inside and nothing she does will ever conceal this fact.

In conclusion, I believe the modern-day dating scene is a minefield and you should avoid it at all cost. I think the risk reward ratio does not favor men and the penalties are extremely high. There are many damaged women who have squandered their youth on sensation seeking activities and now they are dealing with the ramifications of suck reckless behavior. These women have experienced a metaphoric death and have been robbed of their dignity and respect. She lives in misery based on her previous and current actions and the unsuspecting man will only be dragged into her madness. All her sexual experiences live within her and they are driving her mad. The piercings, tattoos, excessive make-up etc. are all means to feel something, even pain if necessary because she knows that she is dead inside.

If you Focus On Health, Success, & Wealth
Women Will Chase You
(Avoid The Red Pill Dope Man)
Part 1

You participated in toxic relationship. You endured mental and physical abuse. She used manipulative shaming tactics and language to subliminally attack your sense justice and morality. She spent a great deal of energy brow beating you with insults about how other men are far superior and you should be thankful she chose you. She demands to be financially compensated and showered with gifts despite the economic hardships that are guaranteed to follow if you comply. She wants access to your bank accounts and credit cards because in her mind this will confirm that you love her. She has been discovered several times sleeping with other men and when you confronted her, she stated that it was all your fault. You failed to do everything she demanded and that pushed her into the arms of other men. Understanding that you are not a violent individual and that the law is on her side when it comes to domestic violence, she graduates to physically assaulting you.

She kicks, punches, bites and scratches you. She throws items like pots and speakers. She begins swinging bats and knives with dangerous intent. You call the police and with your bruises they tell you, the victim to "Take A Walk". She finally grows tired of you and wants to exit the relationship. If you have children, she teams up with the family court as they proceed to gouge you for child support and place you on supervised visitation for an hour with a social worker. If you were married you take a trip to divorce court where she teams up with her divorce lawyer who proceeds to rip your home away from you and force you to pay alimony for a woman you are no longer with. You still get the pleasure of paying the mortgage and as an added bonus, you get to pay her lawyers fees.

This is a situation that replays all over the westernized world and men have attempted to walk away from this madness and seek refuge in the Red Pill Community. They see the horrors of the feminist ideology and the behavior of modern women and they just want to separate themselves from the chaos. They see that the modern-day woman's reckless behavior is promoted and encouraged by the government, the film industry, the music industry, and social media. Many men have taken the red pill to free themselves from the blue-pill shackles of the plantation and take a journey of enlightenment. They seek information that pertains to their situation as a form of therapy. The Red Pill helps them understand what has occurred, acknowledge what they have done, and work on rebuilding themselves. Unfortunately, many men in their journey have encountered, the Red Pill Dope Man. Just like the sleezy preacher that cons entire neighborhoods out of their hard-earned money with feel good words, music, and promises of white Jesus so does the red pill dope man. While men are looking to avoid women, the red pill dope man is looking to get you hooked back on the drug. He tells you that it is your fault that your marriage or relationship ended because "you don't know how to talk to bitches". The Red Pill Dope man states "if you knew how to keep bitches in line none of this would have happened to you". However, not to worry he graciously offers a solution. The Red Pill Dope man promises you an endless supply of female attention and pussy if you just follow these simple steps. Watch this video, buy this CD, join this club and you will be swimming in hoes in no time. They know all the cool lines that will have women going home with you the same night. They can tell you what to say and do to keep women in check and if you follow the steps you will control them. They tell you how to dress and how to walk if you want to attract hoes. They pull you in with the promise of sex and women falling at your feet. All you need to do is buy the starter package but if you act now you will get the intermediate level for 40% off. Your failure with women is based on your ignorance but they will teach you everything you need to know if you just purchase this product.

They are selling you Red Pill Dope and distracting you from the reason you have entered this sector. The intent of this sector was originally to help men acknowledge the egregious sin we have committed is chasing women. Through social conditioning we have been led astray by society and told that she is the prize and should be placed on a pedestal. We have been indoctrinated into a system that has conditioned us to ignore our purpose and pledge our allegiance to women. Societal institutions, corporations, and industry have encouraged men to buy clothing, jewelry, shoes, and cars all to chase women. They have taught us to take our money and go to clubs, lounges, and bars to spend money in the hopes of impressing women. Everything we have ever done has been to impress the opposite sex. This blue pill beta mindset was ingrained in our psyche since we were in grade school. We were constantly bombarded with subliminal and overt messaging. This mental conditioning sent men out into the world with the sole purpose of chasing women. So much so, men began to determine their value and worth on the number of women they could attract or have been with. I recall listening to a stream of a content creator who felt disrespected by criticism another content creator voiced in his direction. The content creator was so livid he made several vlogs in which he challenged the individual to a contest based on how many women they could attract. In a fit of rage, he exclaimed that his game was far superior, and he could "Bag more bitches" than the person he challenged. He even threatened to travel to the other individual's town and accomplish this in his presence.

This helped me to recognize the sad reality that men had been indoctrinated to base their wealth and value on women. This is a self-defeating concept because it is a distraction from pursuing success and wealth. When I was young and attending college, my father helped me get a position with the Department of Education in association with the Department of Corrections. I was 18 years old and was given a position and responsibility that most people could not understand. The money I earned gave me access to things most kids my age could only dream about. I brought jewelry, beepers, two way, pagers, cellphones, name brand clothing, and name brand sneakers. I frequented clubs and spent money because I knew more was coming. I remember one time I lost $150 dollars and just hoped someone who needed it found it. I felt this was because I knew the next morning my bank account would be full. My friends got vehicles before me, but they were hoopties. Both of their cars were junk from the 80's but they were extremely proud to have them. One of them were gifted the car from their dad and the other saved his money to purchase his vehicle. I of course had to purchase a late model vehicle with options because I refused to be caught dead with anything like what they had. During this time, I slept with a lot of girls, did a great deal of partying and hanging out. I remember my father told me that at my young age I was making more than most adults in the city and he was right. A few years later I felt it was time to leave the nest and get my own place. I would have female company often and if not, I was hanging out. We spent a great deal of time impressing females and chasing them. Many of my arguments at that time was based on who attracted better looking women. That was our routine, adding new women to the rotation and bragging about our experiences with them. I was living my best life and felt that nothing would ever top the high I was feeling from my independence. I am making good money and attracting women at such a young age. That is until I got older and realized that I was an idiot.

Looking back at the younger version of myself I sit with regret knowing that I wasted the two most precious aspects of a young man's life. I realized when it was too late that I wasted my time and money. I wasted my money on sneakers, clothes, jewelry, parties, cars, and women. At the same time companies such as Google, Amazon, Microsoft were just beginning to explode as top tier investments. When Amazon went public in 1997 it was worth $18 dollars a share. In 1997 if I would have taken all the money I made and invested at least $10,000 dollars. Today I would have over 1.6 million dollars. I wasted an incredible amount of money and time chasing women. Looking back at my mistakes I know I could have been a millionaire years ago.

So why am I discussing this? Because the Red Pill Dope Man, The Pickup Artist completely disregards the tragedy that brought you to the red pill and attempts to send you right back into the madness. They tell you how to talk to a woman, how to behave, how to walk, how to understand female double speak, and how to dress. On the surface it may appear as if you are learning game. The reality is you are once again being indoctrinated into the teaching that she is the most important thing in your life. You are learning all of these, pick-up artist concepts so you can attempt to attract and control women. The problem is you are once again focused on the same thing that led you to the red pill space. The most important thing you must understand about the red pill space is no one enters this sector in error. To find this ideology you must actively pursue it. It usually happens when you experience some form of heartache or devastation caused by the opposite sex. Your perception and your beliefs are usually shattered by the reality of what is. On Monday you thought you were in a happy marriage with children and a beautiful home. Suddenly you live in a studio apartment on the bad side of town paying child support and alimony. You are no longer allowed to enter the residence you are currently paying the mortgage on but her new man is there. Maybe you were thinking about asking a woman to marry you only to find out that she is sleeping around with multiple men. Possibly you discovered the unfortunate truth that the child that she is having is not yours. There are so many possibilities as to why men land in this sector of social media, but they all involve a traumatic experience with a woman.

The moment you discover this sector your entire world view changes. The things you once held near and dear are irrelevant. You begin to understand you have been living in a false representation of the world and you have been lying to yourself. The moment you learn other men can identify with your situation and you are not alone the pain subsides and you experience red pill rage. The anger is not directed towards women it is mostly directed at yourself. You begin to ask yourself questions like "How could I have been so stupid?" You begin to look at videos and topics and they fit perfectly with what occurred in your life. This is how men start to rebuild the pieces of their lives and develop understanding. They discover the biggest mistake we have made was placing her as the most important fixture in our lives. We use the red pill journey to focus on purpose, health, success, and wealth. We use the ideology to become stronger and avoid the pitfalls that previously trapped us. A man that has lost his home, his children, half his money, and is forced to move in with his family needs to know that while he is in a terrible place many men before him have been there and better days will come. He needs to know that he still has a life to live and if he can focus on being productive and becoming his best self, he will find happiness. The last thing a man needs to hear in this situation is his life imploded because he is a beta. He does not need to hear that he should go to a club and use lines to get chicks. The Red Pill Dope Man uses manipulation tactics and prey on vulnerable men to extract money they are most likely struggling to produce. They make them believe they are the issue and a change in behavior will suddenly make them successful with the ladies. However, you need to by a certain course to learn the secret. What these men are doing is taking advantage of the fragile mental state that many men are experiencing. They are exploiting the learned dependence and need for female companionship. Instead of encouraging these men to focus on self-improvement they push them back into the arms of women. This is time that could be spent on investing, going to the gym, eating healthy, pursuing a passion, or monetizing a talent. Instead, it is wasted on chasing women. They use shaming language and ridicule to keep you hooked on their drug. They tell you that you do not want to participate in the charade because you are:

1. A Beta Male

2. Cannot Get Girls

3. Afraid of Women

4. You are a Loser

5. You are an Incel

6. Your Broke/Poor

These shaming tactics are designed to keep you on the relationship/dating plantation so you can prove your manhood as defined by this group. If these individuals care about you why don't they not encourage men to develop proper diets and exercise? Why do they not promote credible investment opportunities and strategies? Why do they not encourage you to discover your talent and monetize it? The reason is simple. The enlightened man will not fall for the junk the red pill dope man sells. They need you dependent on the drug and focusing on self-improvement is not good for business. I heard a content creator declare that he was providing a business which is very revealing about his intent. If you are looking at your content as a business, then you view the people that patronize your channel as customers which concludes you are for profit. As we all know, the businesses loyalty belongs to the stockholders not the consumer. For example, the tobacco industry knows that the product it sells is deadly and is responsible for the deaths of many of its customers. It knows the product is addictive and causes cancer and they continue to sell the product. Big tobaccos priority is the investor not the customer. The same is true with the fast food industry. McDonald's, Burger King, Wendy's, etc. all know that their product causes diabetes, heart disease, stroke, and cancer. However, this does not prevent them from selling the product because they are for profit and loyal only to stockholders not consumers. The Red Pill Dope Man is selling false hope to vulnerable and desperate men and do not care about the consequences. Many men follow the red pill dope man believing that a few magic lines will attract women and get them laid. Unfortunately, when they discover this is not the case you have men that may fall into depression, drug use, and in more extreme cases may harm themselves or others.

If the red pill dope man really cared about you, he would tell you that a man that is deeply focused on his purpose of achieving health, success, and wealth instantly attracts female attention. The red pill dope man would tell you the man that is driven by developing into the best version of himself is attractive to women. He would tell you happiness truly comes from accomplishment not chasing women. The man that is dedicated to a purpose or achieving a goal is a man that is confident and deserving of respect. If you are worried about what she thinks you have already lost. Women should never be a focal point in your life they should be an accessory. Many men have lost in the game of relationships because this understanding has been stripped away from us by many entities that have a vested interest in our failure. You must consider the reality that the Red Pill Dope Man and other groups are deeply invested in your relationship failures. Your failures and belief in the Red Pill Dope Man ensures that they have a continued and loyal customer.

In conclusion I believe that this male space has unfortunately allowed several individuals motivated by greed to hijack the message to sell red pill dope. Instead of helping men focus on building their health, success, and wealth they have distracted them with promises of an easy lay based on a product of lies. It is important that men understand the most important thing you can do is stay focused on building the best version of yourself. This is done through working on your physical health, your eating habits, and daily routines. Work on your financial health and investments. Make sure you have a purpose; the goal is to become your own boss. Finally, make sure you are working on your mental health. If you focus on these things you will never have an issue attracting women, your biggest issue will be trying to figure out how to keep them away. Focus on yourself, let them focus on you.

If you Focus On Health, Success, & Wealth
Women Will Chase You
(Avoid The Red Pill Dope Man)
Part 2

In our previous chapter we discussed the intent of the red pill dope man and why he wants to distract you from focusing on your purpose, goals, and dreams. We discussed why listening to his advice is counterproductive to self-improvement. We also discussed why it was important you focus on your health, success, and wealth. In this chapter I would like to speak on where your focus should specifically be directed and why. There a very critical aspects of our life that are determined by our health, our behavior, and homeostasis. I think it is very important to discuss these key elements that are essential to building the best version of the self as well as being happy.

Physical Health

Many men are unfortunately facing several health-related issues that are directly related to diet and lack of exercise. According to the Center for Disease Control, obesity affects over 42% of

Americans. They continue to say obesity is linked to type 2 diabetes, heart disease, high blood pressure, stroke, kidney disease, fatty liver disease, sleep apnea, and certain forms of cancer. Based on this information we must be health conscious and not be distracted. Health is closely related to success and wealth because it speaks to discipline. A disciplined man is not impulsive and is able to resist immediate gratification. This mindset will have an impact on all aspects of his life which will be a key component to his overall success. In a study referenced by the Center for Disease Control it was cited that educated and/or successful individuals were less likely to become overweight or obese. While this is not absolute, it does point to a pattern of discipline amongst one group as opposed to another. This is evidence that many individuals doom themselves to poverty based on weight and mindset. Many people in poverty-stricken communities and the working poor suffer from health-related issues based on weight and eating habits. I understand that many of them are forced to make food selections based on budget, but health plays such a critical role in success and wealth. There are many alternatives that are possible, even in poverty. However, many people seek a quick solution to their issues which is usually the worst decision. The undisciplined mind easily gives into unhealthy urges and is unable to make sound decisions. That trip to McDonalds, Burger King, & KFC is killing you. You lack the will power to resist the saturated fats, cholesterol and other bad elements contributing to your weight gain. At the same time, this mindset is taking you off your purpose. The excess weight contributes to fatigue which drains your ability to pursue your passions, projects, or business ventures. The weight gain and unhealthy eating keeps you from tapping into your energy. The excessive weight gain prevents you from having clear thoughts and following through on your intent. You always procrastinate and as a result nothing ever gets done. You say "I will do it tomorrow" or "I will start next week" but it never happens. The chemicals in the bad foods we eat destroy our will power and our drive to excel. It leaves us in a sloth like state rationalizing our failures with excuses.

I can speak to this specifically, I allowed food to impede my progress. Some years ago, I received a health scare that I was pre-diabetic. To add to this, I lost my father due to health-related issues based on a poor diet and lack of exercise. My father was a correction officer so most of his time was spent in the facility. One of the things most people do not understand about a Correction Officer position is it requires mandatory overtime. This means that without warning you can be mandated to stay for a double or even a triple shift. Something that is rarely discussed is people who work in these positions often have health issue due to poor diet and exercise. My father was no exception and the nightly runs to the pizza, Chinese, burger joints etc. finally caught up to him when he needed to be rushed to the hospital after he fainted while on duty. My father developed several heath issues and they were all directly related to his diet and lack of exercise. Unfortunately, he lost his battle in 2014 however, it became clear that we needed to make better health choices and walk away from the temptation of fast food and high calories. Despite the loss of my father the situation did not become real for me until I was told in 2017 by my doctor, I was pre-diabetic. I remember that day in late October and the fear that came over me. The memory of my father a few years ago in a hospital bed, a prisoner to heart disease and diabetes. The greater fear being that it would soon be my turn to take his place in that hospital bed. If I suddenly became diagnosed as diabetic, I would have no one to blame but myself. My body warned me in several ways that this process of self-destruction was well underway. I began to experience heart burn and had trouble digesting food. It felt as if I did not fully complete a bowel movement which was always uncomfortable. I began to have trouble sleeping because it felt as if the acid in my stomach was attempting to come up my esophagus. Not to mention the soreness I felt after sleeping. I decided at that moment I would just stop eating food. I know it sounds extreme but that is exactly what I did, I just stopped eating food. I went to the store and purchased a bunch of fruit and some vegetables and began to blend it until it became juice. Anytime I was hungry I would drink my blended concoction. Whenever I did not want to chop up fruit, I would buy the freshly cut bowls of fruit from my local supermarket and turn those into juice. That was my only food source for months. In just three to four months I lost so much weight my six pack came back and so did the wings under my chest. With the extra weight gone I became extremely energetic and active. I kept a routine of going to the gym and working on my projects. I started investing my money and my outlook on life was much more positive. I am not a doctor so I cannot suggest you assume the diet that I did, however I do suggest you start to stay away from the bad foods. Look to a diet of fruits, vegetables, lean meats, and very little starch items. To fight hunger, I would suggest water and green tea as they have been known to fight the urge to reach for bad foods. You must protect your body from the harmful chemicals. I would also suggest using a supplement as directed of products that focus on colon cleansing. These types of products are designed to remove the waste in the colon and intestine that have been sitting inside your body for years. They work to remove as much waste a possible from your body and can help to prevent health disorders and possibly some cancers. I speak of these things because we need to be health conscious. I lost my father and almost faced similar health issue because I ignored the importance of a healthy body and I want to prevent our brotherhood from having the same experience.

Mental Health (Relationships)

Relationships in the modern age are a dangerous venture to pursue. It seems with the rise of feminism and the blue-pill mindset that is prevalent in law, media, and entertainment, relationships have absolutely no benefit for men. Contemplating entering a relationship in this modern era can and will be a strain on your mental health. I think many men have not realized that society itself is not well. However, in an asylum where the patients are in charge the rational person is considered insane. Make no mistake the modern male has everything working against his best interest and his failure to recognize the danger will be his demise. You live in a world of #metoo, believe all women, and all sex is rape. Your world is dominated by the abortion is birth control crowd. If they want to kill the child there is nothing you can do about as the father, but if she wants to keep it and the father does not, he is forced to pay for 18 years. This is the crowd that believes if you are an overweight man you are lazy and disgusting. However, if you are a woman and overweight you are healthy at any size. The point of all of this is women have gained control of the system and have become drunk with power. A relationship at this juncture is a journey into madness. The modern woman serves no purpose in a man's life. She does not cook, clean, or wash clothes because she believes it is a sign of patriarchy and demeaning to women. To merely suggest it makes you a misogynist who seeks to imprison women in a life of servitude. You live in a time in which a woman that sleeps around is celebrated. A promiscuous woman is no longer perceived as a negative trait. A woman that has been with many men is finding herself, or exploring, or having experiences. If you decide that you want a woman that has very little sexual experience, they label you as an out of touch loser who has unrealistic expectations. In this modern age you must acknowledge that there is no incentive for the modern woman to remain loyal to you. There are no societal, legal, or personal repercussions for her behavior. In fact, if you discover your wife or girlfriend is cheating on you, she has the right to blame you for her behavior. It is something you did or did not do to make her go out and sleep with other men. On the other hand, if you sleep with other women you are a piece of garbage who does not deserve to be with a good woman.

The point is, pursuing a relationship at this juncture is against your best interest. The modern woman does not receive enjoyment from a happy healthy relationship based on trust and respect. They derive pleasure from chaos, confusion, and dysfunction. She is not looking for stability, she is looking for an emotional rollercoaster. She seeks to constantly attack your mental health by employing manipulation and gaslighting techniques to keep you in constant doubt. She enjoys turmoil and she seek to make you question everything you believe. She enjoys the arguments, the physical fights, police involvement, making a scene, the cheating and many other things that will cause conflict. She wants to see you in distress. She wants to see you make mistakes and possibly throw you off your game. She wants you to be distracted and she seeks to cause interference anyway she can. She wants to drain your resources, not out of necessity but just to see if she can. She will want shoes, clothes, make-up, and jewelry. She will constantly want to eat at restaurants and go to events. Her goal will be to spend as much of your money as she can leaving your financial capabilities depleted. The modern woman does not have your best interest at heart. She is not interested in building a solid foundation to help generation wealth. The modern woman only wants to take from your bottom line. She tells you that she wants to be with a wealthy man because she does not want to work. She does not have any meaningful goals; she wants things the easiest way possible. We currently live in a society where women can become famous for nothing so there is no drive for them to become better people. She will be celebrated for making a sex tape so she will use that to trap men for their money. The modern woman will distract you from your purpose and use manipulation, chaos and confusion to cause harm to your mental health. She will make you think things are not true, tell lies, and spread disinformation. She will devour you in her madness and enjoy watching you lose your grip on reality. She is damaged and she wants you to share in her misery. A relationship will not allow you to excel in your dreams and goals in these modern times, it will be a hindrance to your forward momentum. If you are a man seeking health, success, and wealth your best option is to remain single and focused on the task at hand.

Careers & Entrepreneurship

Many men are blessed with great potential but unfortunately many of us never get to bring our talents into fruition. Many men are living unfulfilled lives based on the reality they fail to pursue their purpose. Some men work in fields that they loath while others simply do not know how to get started on the path to their destiny. In many cases many men are forced into jobs that they despise and are distracted or even discouraged from pursuing a better a career, business venture, or entrepreneurial endeavors by a girlfriend or wife. This unfortunate scenario has occurred all throughout history and continues to do so today. The man that allows himself to be distracted by relationships will always lose focus on building a foundation. Chasing women is a time-consuming activity so other aspects of your life must suffer, and they do. It is only when time has passed you by that you realize what you have allowed to slip away. Women seem to be a very strong influence in our failures because it is their voice you hear when you make life altering decisions. While most men can think about the future and develop a vision, most women are only concerned with the immediate future. If given the option, they seek comfort even if it means missing out on greater rewards for being patient. To help you better understand this concept think of a man who wants to build a car that runs on regular water. His girlfriend or wife will constantly nag him and even tell him that it is a stupid idea to get him to abandon his vision. Why? Because she needs him to focus on a job, something that brings in a paycheck every week. Money right now is value to her. She cannot see the reality in terms of if he is successful, they will be billionaires. So, let's say her nagging wears him down he throws the blueprints in the garbage and his next-door neighbor finds them and successfully builds the car. The woman that nagged her boyfriend for trying to do the same thing will leave him for the neighbor that built used his blueprint. My point is she does not care about the future benefits she is only concerned about immediate extraction of resources.

Therefore, men must focus on their needs and wants. What she wants is in direct conflict of your goals and in most cases does not benefit you. I want to encourage men to start looking in areas and activities that will help you build a solid foundation in careers and/or entrepreneurial ventures.

A) College (Stem Programs ONLY) – I do not support nor condone college. I believe that it is a government scam designed to keep you in debt for most of your life. With that said, If You believe you really need to pursue this path the only exception, would be a STEM program. Going to college for anything related to Science, Technology, Engineering, and Mathematics can and will lead to some very lucrative opportunities for you. There is no place in the world that is not in need of more individuals in the STEM program. They have very high demand and very high pay because of it. These skills can also translate into business ventures.

B) Vocational School – I think many men should focus on vocational school because in many ways it is a gateway to freedom. I think Vocational schools provide men with skills and abilities needed to walk off the plantation. You Can Learn Auto Repair, Computer Science, Plumbing, Heating & Air, and many other things. With the type of skills, you learn in a vocational setting you can take them anywhere in the world with you. You can also use these skills to start a business.

C) Online Careers – This is the best time for young men to pursue careers online. In this modern age there are so many ways to monetize your talents and passions. For instance, if you play video games you can turn that pastime into a lucrative career by starting a YouTube, Twitch, or Facebook Games Account. This will allow you to do what you love while reaching an audience that will financially support you. If you are an exceptional player, you can join the e-sports or major league gaming circuit and compete for cash pools all while building a brand. You can also use social media platforms to monetize your other talents as well. For instance, if you are an artist you can reach millions with designs, logos, etc. If you do music there is Spotify, Sound Cloud, Apple music and you can have your music posted there. There have never been more opportunities for men to create and become their own boss based solely on their talent. You can literally create content about anything and if you put the effort into the project you will be able to monetize it. If you are a writer, Amazon has made it possible to publish your book on their site. You can even convert it to an audio book. There are so many possibilities and the best part about it is that you are your own boss. For Men who do not wish to pursue the entrepreneurial route but want to monetize skills they have acquired from vocational and/or college settings there are apps to help you connect with part-time and full time work to provide income. You can also become an independent contractor with companies and set your own hours.

Investing

As you gentlemen know, my YouTube & Patreon family are known as the #Cryptogang. I decided to move forward with this concept because many men especially melanated men fail to invest in their futures due to the distraction of material and women. Many men spend fortunes on material that are depreciating assets and women who only extract their resources. The #Cryptogang is a rallying cry to urge men to focus on investments. We specifically encourage men to investigate gold, silver, and cryptocurrency because of their ability to generate wealth. Gold and silver have been on a steady increase as we see a society that is beginning to move away from fiat currency into a digital format. However, we must add that the emergence of cryptocurrency has opened a new door to prosperity in many respects. I am not a financial advisor and I cannot advise you on which cryptocurrencies to pursue. I must ask you to do your due diligence as well as seek a financial professional if possible. With that said I can say that crypto is the wave of the future. China,

Russia, and now the United States are in the process of creating and releasing a form of cryptocurrency. Mark Zuckerberg of Facebook attempted to release his own cryptocurrency. In 2017 we saw bitcoin go from $100 dollars to $20,000 dollars. The incredible thing is the crypto market is still in its infancy stage. It is only worth between 250 billion to 300 Billion while the stock market is worth more than 30 Trillion dollars. This means that the crypto market is not even 1% of the current stock market. It has excellent potential to grow and it is my belief the earlier people adopt this market the better chance they will have to become wealthy. I believe the society is moving towards a cashless format. With that said digital currency is the new money. This is ground zero and I believe we all have an opportunity to build wealth through this avenue.

Conclusion

The modern man must be responsible and develop routines that speak to his mental, physical, and financial health. We must be disciplined and focused to build generational wealth. We can no longer be distracted by things that produce no value and we must avoid immediate gratification. We must understand the modern women is a detriment to what we seek to accomplish. Chasing women in modern times is a fruitless venture. Focus on creating the best version of yourself to truly be happy.

The End

Made in the USA
Monee, IL
07 October 2021